Table of Contents

GW00648559

The Giver of Peace

Tim Britton

Published by Tim Britton, 2023.

THE GIVER OF PEACE

First edition. October 3, 2023.

Copyright © 2023 Tim Britton.

ISBN: 979-8223681496

Written by Tim Britton.

This book is dedicated to my wife Frances, with great gratitude for all her love and patience!

INTRODUCTION

How do I find peace with God? Or freedom from guilt? What hope is there for the future? How can I be sure of God's love for me? Paul answers these questions (and more) in his letter to the Romans, a letter that has given comfort and hope to millions in the 2000 or so years since it was written, and has transformed the lives of many, including such great reformers as St Augustine, Martin Luther, and John Wesley.

I first engaged with Paul's letter to the Romans at Dundee University Christian Union. I was an undergraduate in the Science department, intending to do the general science first year and then switch to the medical department if I could. All my life until then I'd wanted to be a doctor, but sport was much more attractive than school work and my grades weren't good enough to get into the best medical schools I had applied for, so Dundee was my preferred option B. Someone from my old school was also there, and he invited me to come to the Christian Union meetings. The theme of that first term was the book of Romans, with each speaker expected to go through succeeding passages verse by verse, explaining what it meant and how it was relevant.

I had been brought up in a Christian home, and had been sent with my two brothers (twins) to a boarding school with a Christian foundation. (My father worked in Nigeria, where my twin sister and I were born.) When I was eighteen my father gave me William

Temple's 'Readings in St John's Gospel' to read, and it was the story of doubting Thomas which made me realise I was not committed to Christ. Thomas refused to believe Jesus had risen from the dead until he saw him for himself; when he saw him, he said "My Lord and my God". I knew I could not say that. I believed Jesus was Lord and God, but to call him 'my' Lord was something else, and I could not do it. At eighteen I wanted to be in control of my life. For several months I lived a lie, knowing the truth but refusing to live by it, until one evening around my nineteenth birthday I suddenly felt that now was the time. I had to commit myself to Jesus. I did so: I knelt down by my bed and gave myself to Jesus – and immediately had a strong sense that he had heard and accepted me, I now belonged to him and he would look after me for the rest of my life and on into the next.

However, despite regular church-going, I knew very little about the Christian life. That first meeting of the Christian Union I attended opened my eyes to what was for me a new world, the world of the Bible. The speaker was William Still from Aberdeen, and I was transfixed by the teaching of Romans 5, his subject for that evening. Since then the letter to the Romans has been foundational for me, and its teaching has been something I have tried to pass on through my nearly forty years' ministry as a Church of England vicar, including a spell as a mission partner in Uganda. (How these changes came about is another story.)

These reflections are simply a record of some of my thoughts as I consider Paul's teaching and try to apply it to my life. They are not intended as a verse-by-verse commentary, nor are they in any way scholarly – my explanations of what Paul is saying are my attempt to make sense of them in my own mind, and are not authoritative! If at times it seems a bit 'preachy', please forgive me; I am preaching primarily to myself. I offer them to others in the hope that they may be helpful – as much by stimulating thought which might lead to different conclusions as by bringing new insights or confirming old ones. If they in any way grow faith and draw people closer to Jesus, I will be happy!

The text of Paul's letter to the Romans, and other New Testament Scriptures quoted in this book, are from the Open English Bible, release 2020.2 (which is free of copyright restrictions), unless otherwise stated. Quotations from the Old Testament are from the World English Bible (public domain).

I am grateful to my wife Frances, and to my friend David Orsborne, for their proof-reading and suggestions. Any remaining errors and awkward sentences are entirely my responsibility!

4

ROMANS CHAPTER 1

¹From Paul, a servant of Jesus Christ, who has been called to become an apostle, and has been set apart to tell God's good news.

Paul's letter to the Romans is all about God's good news – about peace with God through Jesus Christ. God is the giver of peace: a harmonious relationship with him is not something that is deserved or can be earned; it is a gift, a gift of love, as Paul will make clear throughout this letter. It is a gift that will eventually extend to the whole creation, but it begins with us. Paul's calling from God is to tell this good news to those who haven't heard it. Some in Rome had heard it, but Paul wants to visit them, and in this letter he spells out the details of what he preaches in order to prepare the way. So he begins by introducing himself.

'Paul, a servant of Jesus Christ'. Those few words carry so much meaning. A servant of Jesus Christ is a position of the highest honour! The word 'Christ' is a title, meaning 'anointed one' – in other words, a king or a priest, or both. Jesus is the Messiah (the Hebrew word for Christ), the king promised by God who would rescue his people, end all evil, and bring perfect peace and harmony to the whole world for ever. To be his servant in this amazing task is a huge privilege! However, the word 'servant' in the Greek is also the word for 'slave', someone who is the property of another.

How could anyone happily describe themselves as a 'slave' of Jesus Christ? Isn't that demeaning? Yet that chimes in with my own experience (see the Introduction), and, far from feeling demeaned, I feel affirmed and comforted. If I am Jesus' property, that means he is responsible for me, and I know enough about Jesus from the gospels to know that he values me, loves me and wants the best for me. He is my shepherd, who looks after me and loves me, as described in Psalm 23 and in John 10 vs11, 28-29. To be his servant gives meaning and purpose to my life; he authorises me to act in his name! I take to heart what Paul told the Colossians, 'Whatever you say or do, do everything in the name of the Lord Jesus.' It's true that if I am his 'slave' I have no right to say 'No' to him; but it is equally true that I am his slave voluntarily, and that I am fully able to choose whether or not to obey him, whatever the rights and wrongs may be. I have chosen to obey him, and I believe that every follower of Jesus Christ needs to be fully committed to him as their own personal Lord and God. Anything less is surely an attempt to serve two masters, which Jesus says is impossible. Yet how often do I fail to obey!

However, full commitment does not guarantee perfect obedience. When I first gave myself to Jesus I thought that I was duty bound to go and preach the gospel while living by faith, like the first disciples. I got a suitcase together with warm clothing, hitch-hiked from Thanet in Kent (south-east England) as far as Leeds (northern England), spent half the night with all my warm clothes on in a snowy field and the other half taking shelter in a public toilet, then instead of hitchhiking to Scotland to evangelise the natives as I had planned I hitchhiked home to Sussex! That was the end of my first missionary journey! What I would have preached I have no idea! I thought I was proving my commitment to Christ, when I was really proving I had a lot to learn. And I am still learning.

Paul knew from the time he first met Jesus that he was called to be an 'apostle' – one sent by God – and that he had been chosen specially to share the good news with those who were not Jewish as he was. (We read an account of his call in Acts 8.) I believe that was a special task, not one for every Christian. However, every Christian prays for God's kingdom to come, and for his will to be done on earth as in heaven, and if that is our desire we will naturally want to play our part to make it happen. What that means will vary from Christian to Christian, as we follow the guidance of the Holy Spirit.

²This good news God promised long ago through his prophets in the sacred scriptures, ³concerning his Son, Jesus Christ, our Lord; who, as to his human nature, was descended from David, ⁴but, as to the spirit of holiness within him, was miraculously designated Son of God by his resurrection from the dead.

WHAT IS GOD'S GOOD news? Paul does not elaborate here – he will do so in the rest of the letter. But he does want to make a point that was very important to him and to the whole early church, that the good news was something foretold centuries beforehand in the Jewish holy Scriptures, our Old Testament. I wish I knew exactly what Scriptures he and the other apostles had in mind – presumably ones Jesus had pointed out to them in the days between his resurrection and ascension (Luke 24:27,45-47).

Some of these Scriptures are quoted again and again in the New Testament, or are ones we can easily identify – such as Psalms 2, 22, 110, Isaiah 7:14, Isaiah 9:6-7, Isaiah 53, Isaiah 61:1-3. These were written hundreds of years before Jesus. In all those years people waited, and like today many must have thought they were just words; but in God's good time they were fulfilled, often in amazing detail. I am amazed how many Christians find the Old Testament irrelevant – yet it was Jesus' and the early church's Bible, recognised as being inspired by God.

The good news is all about Jesus. It is good news of peace with God; but that peace comes only through a person, Jesus of Nazareth, born of Mary, recognised as a descendant of King David who had been promised by God that a descendant would always be on his throne. Jesus was 'designated' or 'appointed' Son of God in power by his resurrection. This appointment was not the time when he became the divine Son of God (he had always been that, as God said at his baptism); it was the time when he as a human being, the first with the new resurrection body, was designated 'Son of God' and given all authority in heaven and earth – as a human being!

> [5]Through him we received the gift of the apostolic office, to win submission to the faith among all nations for the glory of his name. [6]And among these nations are you – you who have been called to belong to Jesus Christ.

[7]To all in Rome who are dear to God and have been called to become Christ's people, may God, our Father, and the Lord Jesus Christ bless you and give you peace.

PAUL NOW MENTIONS A bit more about his calling as an apostle. The apostolic office was a gift of Jesus, the foremost gift according to Paul's list in 1 Corinthians 12:28, and as a gift was not something that could be earned or deserved. Paul certainly knew he didn't deserve it, having received the gift while on the road to persecute the church in Damascus! However, his apostolic gift was for a particular purpose, to 'win submission to the faith among all nations' (literally 'for obedience of faith'). I would have expected him to say something more positive, like 'to preach the good news of Jesus to all nations'. But Paul is very much aware that the good news of salvation through Jesus is only good news if the hearer responds with faith in Jesus. He is the Lord, the Messiah, the Saviour who, 'by the exercise of his power to bring everything into subjection to himself, ...will make our humble bodies like his glorious body' (Philippians 3:21). Salvation is not only about forgiveness, though that is an important part of it. It is about transformation, transformation of the whole of creation – including us. And that transformation involves submission to Jesus as the Lord we obey – a submission that is the result and proof of our faith in him. Faith in Jesus as Saviour without submission to him as Lord is not really faith in Jesus. Paul's work was to reach out to all nations, not just Israel, and that was why he wanted to visit Rome.

'For the glory of his name': the 'name' of Jesus is the label for all he is – his nature, his character, his purpose; Paul's work was to proclaim all that Jesus was and did, so that people would believe in him as he truly is, and give him the honour that he is due. I think this little phrase reveals Paul's primary motivation: it was not for personal reward, nor even for the sake of humanity – though that was God's motivation in sending Jesus, according to John 3:16 – it was for the glory of Jesus. Why was that so important to Paul? And why was God's honour so important to Jesus, that the first request in the Lord's prayer is for God's name to be hallowed, honoured and revered? I think the answer must be, 'Because they deserve it.' And the number one reason (among many) that Jesus and God deserve it must be because of their amazing love shown to the human race which does not deserve such love, as Paul will go on to show. Paul is a recipient of that love, and knows it; and he wants the whole world to receive it and know it too. How important is the glory of God and the glory of Jesus to me?

In this letter Paul is writing to people in Rome who were among those who had believed the good news of Jesus, and were therefore dear to God as are all Christians. He does not say when or how they had received the good news; we can only assume it was through contact with ordinary Christians in the course of daily life. There is no mention in the New Testament of any of the apostles visiting Rome, though residents of Rome were among those who had heard Peter preaching on that day of Pentecost (Acts 2). However they came to faith, this letter is addressed to them, and he ends the address section of his letter with a blessing – not the customary 'Peace be with you' but an expanded version. Paul links God the Father with the Lord Jesus Christ, who together give blessing and peace – possibly having in mind Jesus' words, "The Father and I are one" (John 10:30).

[8]First, I thank my God through Jesus Christ for you all, because the report of your faith is spreading throughout the world. [9]God, to whom I offer the worship of my soul as I tell the good news of his Son, is my witness how constantly I mention you when I pray, [10]asking that, if he be willing, I may some day at last find the way open to visit you. [11]For I long to see you, in order to impart to you some spiritual gift and so give you fresh strength – [12]or rather that both you and I may find encouragement in each other's faith. [13]I want you to know, my friends, that I have many times intended coming to see you – but until now I have been prevented – that I might find among you some fruit of my labours, as I have already among the other nations. [14]I have a duty to both the Greek and the barbarian, to both the cultured and the ignorant. [15]And so, for my part, I am ready to tell the good news to you also who are in Rome.

IN ALMOST ALL HIS LETTERS Paul begins with thanks and praise to God. He often tells his readers to be thankful, and sets a great example. He thanks God for salvation through Jesus Christ; he praises his readers for their faith and love, and gives thanks for their support and encouragement. Even when things are going badly, he finds something to be thankful for. That is something I know I have to learn from – and not to give thanks just as a matter of duty, but from the heart.

In this particular letter Paul thanks God for the Roman Christians' faith that he's heard about. (The 'world' is the world he knows, the Roman empire.) But this leads him straight away to the main purpose of the letter: to let them know that he hopes to visit them in order to build up their faith. He turns his hope into prayer, not just once but often. Paul is a thankful person, and he is also a prayerful person, and is very open about it as we see in so many of his letters. 'To whom I offer the worship of my soul' is literally 'whom I serve in my spirit'; his service of God as an apostle of Jesus is from the heart, not just a matter of going through the motions. Is my service of God from the heart? I would like to think so, but the truthful answer would probably be, 'Not always'. The spirit is willing, but the flesh is weak!

In saying he wants to visit the Romans, Paul does not want them to feel patronised; he knows that he will be encouraged while encouraging them. My family and I went to Uganda as mission partners from 1983 to 1988. I was involved in teaching people who were going to be church leaders; but while I had a ministry of teaching, I and my family learnt so much from the people we were living among, especially from their faith in very difficult circumstances. I'm sure that was Paul's experience too when planting new churches. But Paul also knew he had a lot to give. And Rome was the centre of the Roman world; if the good news of Jesus was to take proper root, it had to take root in Rome also.

¹⁶For I am not ashamed of the good news; it is the power of God which brings salvation to everyone who believes, to the Jew first, but also to the Greek. ¹⁷For in it there is a revelation of the divine righteousness

resulting from faith and leading on to faith; as scripture says – "Through faith the righteous will find life."

PAUL WANTS TO SHARE the gospel – the good news of Jesus. He cannot keep it secret, as if it were something to be ashamed about. It is amazing good news – and when it is shared God's power works through the message to bring salvation to everyone who hears it and believes it. Paul knew that Jesus was the Jewish Messiah, and his own people should hear the news first. But the prophetic Scriptures had foretold that the Messiah would be a light for non-Jews as well (the word 'Greek' stands for all non-Jews). For in the good news of salvation the righteousness of God is revealed to all humanity, so all can see not only just how good and loving God is, but also how we can become good and loving ourselves. 'Righteousness' in Paul's writings is not just a matter of being good; more importantly, it is a matter of being in a good relationship with God. Goodness comes into it, of course – we need to know that God is good, and God needs to know that we are fit for a relationship with him. But that relationship cannot depend on our obedience to God, as Paul will later explain. It depends on our faith – on our believing the good news, and responding to it wholeheartedly. That's what the rest of this letter is all about.

As I read this, I feel challenged about my own passion for sharing the good news of Jesus. I am a buttoned-up Brit – I don't want to be a 'Bible Basher', or to share my deep beliefs with people who don't want to know. Yet I belong to a church tradition where 'evangelism' (sharing the good news) is vitally important and we are all encouraged to heed Jesus' great commission to the church to 'Go and make disciples of all nations' (Matthew 28:19), starting with our own friends and neighbours. So I pray for my friends and neighbours, and long for them to hear the good news; and I ask God to give me opportunities to share my faith naturally and in an unthreatening and respectful way. I have opportunities when preaching in church, of course – and when Paul went to a new place he usually started sharing the message in a place where Jews and other interested people met for worship. I occasionally have conversations in which my work as a church leader comes up, but rarely does that lead into questions about my beliefs, and I feel diffident about opening up the subject without some positive encouragement to do so. Yet if the gospel is the power of God bringing salvation to all who believe, shouldn't I be more forthcoming? And if so, how can I share the good news of Jesus without putting people off? I am not an apostle nor an evangelist, both of whom have a God-given calling to evangelise with gifts to match; yet Paul told Timothy to 'do the work of an evangelist', which implies that was not Timothy's primary gift. I have not seen many people come to faith in Jesus through my conversation and way of life, though there have been one or two; nor does it often happen in my preaching, with some notable exceptions in Uganda a long time ago. But how passionate am I now? More to the point: do I truly believe that if and when I share the gospel, God's power for salvation is at work? Even when my words are not as persuasive as I would wish? After all, it's God's power, not my words, that brings salvation!

¹⁸So, too, there is a revelation from heaven of the divine wrath against every form of ungodliness and wickedness on the part of those people who, by their wicked lives,

are stifling the truth. [19]This is so, because what can be known about God is plain to them; for God himself has made it plain. [20]For ever since the creation of the universe God's invisible attributes – his everlasting power and divinity – are to be seen and studied in his works, so that people have no excuse; [21]because, although they learned to know God, yet they did not offer him as God either praise or thanksgiving. Their speculations about him proved futile, and their undiscerning minds were darkened. [22]Professing to be wise, they showed themselves fools; [23]and they transformed the glory of the immortal God into the likeness of mortal humans, and of birds, and beasts, and reptiles.

PAUL NOW TURNS TO THE main topic of his letter, the good news of Jesus. The good news is all about salvation, but that would not be good news for us unless we knew what we needed to be saved from, and that is what Paul begins with.

In a word, we need to be saved from the wrath of God. His wrath is revealed in Scripture, in God's warnings and God's action against evil-doers. Paul tells us that God has revealed his anger against every form of ungodliness and wickedness. That's a difficult message to hear. We would be happy if God was angry with wickedness – aren't we all? But ungodliness? Why is that a problem? After all, there are many people who do not believe in God yet live lives full of love and goodness. But Paul states that by their wickedness they are stifling the truth, the truth about God. Good people who misrepresent God, or deny his existence or relevance, encourage others to follow their example even if they don't mean to. Even before his conversion, Paul would have agreed with Jesus that the first and greatest commandment is to love God with all our heart and mind and strength; so anything that goes against that commandment is wicked indeed. It would not be so wicked if there was no evidence for God's existence and nature, but that evidence has been there ever since the creation of the world, he says. The creation itself, the world we live in, shows God's everlasting power and divinity, so those who deny his existence have no excuse.

But is that fair? Lots of philosophers have attempted to prove the existence of God without much success, and the writer to the Hebrews says clearly it is by faith we understand that the world was formed at God's command. If it could be proved, faith would not be necessary. But Paul's point is not that people suppress the truth about God by their logic, but by their wickedness – people do not want to believe in a God who deserves to be obeyed, let alone loved. In his day nothing was known about evolution and the origins of the universe; all cultures had some explanation about the beginning of the world, and that explanation usually, if not always, involved a god or gods. God or gods were thought by many to be involved in everyday life, and needed to be appeased or invoked. Human beings seem to have had a religious streak in their nature from the earliest days; and also have a sense about what is and what is not fair and just. Yet their beliefs about the world did not give rise to a sense of dependency and thanksgiving for whatever good they enjoyed, and the awesomeness of nature did not result in praise to its creator. And that is still the case today for many people – they believe there is 'something' there, but do not give that 'something' the praise and thanks that is deserved. And Paul says they are 'stifling the truth'.

Paul tells us that 'what can be known about God is plain to them; for God himself has made it plain. For ever since the creation of the universe God's invisible attributes – his everlasting power and divinity – are to be seen and studied in his works, so that people have no excuse'. God's creation reveals important truths about God, and is there for all with spiritual eyes to see. Do modern scientific theories and discoveries rule out any involvement of a God or gods in the formation of the world? No. An explanation of how something was manufactured, or how a biological process works, doesn't rule out the existence of a maker. The awe and wonder I feel at some natural phenomenon – or some human achievement – is not nullified by my understanding of the processes involved, and I gladly praise God for them. But if I refuse to see anything beyond those processes, and refuse to believe in the possibility of invisible realities in addition to the visible, then that is my deliberate decision, for which I can be held to account. I need to be open to inconvenient truths! Does that openness include being open to the possibility that Paul's God does not exist? To my mind, only if it can be proved that the resurrection of Jesus from the dead did not happen and all the evidence for it discounted – and none have succeeded in that, though many have tried.

Paul wanted everyone to see the glory of God in creation. But instead he saw temples full of idols, statues of people or animals or birds which were the focus of people's worship. How could people think those were adequate representations of God, worthy of their worship? He knew that God hated such things. The ten commandments included a prohibition of idol worship, and Jewish history showed that disobedience in that matter resulted in their exile from the land God had given them.

I am encouraged by these verses to look afresh at God's creation, and to learn from it more about God. Jesus often illustrated his teaching from the world around him. Those with eyes to see, let them see! A friend who became a Christian said his conversion was like replacing a black-and-white television with a colour one – in a way, nothing had changed, none of his questions were answered, yet life now seemed so vivid!

[24]Therefore God abandoned them to impurity, letting them follow the cravings of their hearts, until they dishonoured their own bodies; [25]for they had substituted a lie for the truth about God, and had reverenced and worshipped created things more than the Creator, who is to be praised for ever. Amen. [26]That, I say, is why God abandoned them to degrading passions. Even the women among them perverted the natural use of their bodies to the unnatural; [27]while the men, disregarding that for which women were intended by nature, were consumed with passion for one another. Men indulged in vile practices with men, and incurred in their own persons the inevitable penalty for their perverseness.

[28]Then, as they would not keep God before their minds, God abandoned them to depraved thoughts, so that

they did all kinds of shameful things. [29]They revelled in every form of wickedness, evil, greed, vice. Their lives were full of envy, murder, quarrelling, treachery, malice. [30]They became back-biters, slanderers, impious, insolent, boastful. They devised new sins. They disobeyed their parents. [31]They were undiscerning, untrustworthy, without natural affection or pity. [32]Well aware of God's decree, that those who do such things deserve to die, not only are they guilty of them themselves, but they even applaud those who do them.

HERE I SEE BOTH THE nature of God's wrath and the nature of the prevailing culture of Paul's day.

God's wrath does not lead immediately to the penalty deserved by the wicked person (death, v.32). Instead, 'God abandoned them,' gave them up. Three times Paul uses that expression. God has given people freedom of choice, and so he lets them follow their own desires and do what they want to do, however vile and degrading they are. But freedom brings consequences, and God lets them suffer whatever the natural consequences are. Paul does not say what these consequences were, and there is no point in speculating. The notable point is that God's wrath has an element of grace in it: God gives time for people to change and respond to the good news of Jesus, and continues to provide for them. Even in the Old Testament, when we read of God punishing evil-doers, we also see that lots of evil-doers are allowed to continue their evil ways. God's wrath is revealed, surprisingly to me, in his letting nature take its course and not interfering – at least, not often. The time will come when God says 'Enough', and all of us will be called to account and receive the due reward for our decisions, as Paul says in the next chapter.

The things people in that culture practised were, in Paul's eyes, degrading and shameful. Many of what Paul lists are sexual in nature, but not all. Greed, envy, quarrelling, back-biting, boastfulness, disobedience to parents, untrustworthiness – these and more are features of every human society. The root of all these things, he says, is the 'cravings of their hearts'. Paul believed those who did them knew that it was wrong – they were 'well aware of God's decree, that those who do such things deserve to die'. How did they know? Paul does not say. Perhaps he was thinking of the general knowledge people had of the Jewish religion and standards; or maybe he was thinking of the innate sense of fairness that we all have, which appeals against all abuse or misuse of ourselves or of other people, activity done 'without natural affection or pity' but mainly to satisfy one's own lusts or pride.

Our culture is different from that of ancient Rome. Two of the sins in this list would be questioned today. Disobedience to parents is not regarded as such a heinous sin as it was in the Bible – the fifth of the ten commandments is the command to obey our parents, and Paul points out to the Ephesians that it is the first commandment with a promise. There may well be occasions when parents command their children to do ungodly acts; wouldn't disobedience then be a Christian duty? I remember such a discussion in my church youth group when I was a teenager! I don't remember the conclusion; hopefully it was that we can continue to respect and honour our parents as the ones through whom God has given us life and our genetic inheritance, even if our homes have been unhappy ones, and even when we feel we have to disobey them for the sake of God's kingdom. I say this, though I have not experienced anything but good parenting. That reminds me of an incident when we were on leave from Uganda. I visited a church as part of my CMS duties, and went to a home group where they offered to pray for me. Someone felt that I needed prayer about my relationship with my father – he had worked in Nigeria for most of my childhood and so had been an absent father for long stretches of time. I didn't feel I needed that prayer – I had been proud of his work, and didn't feel any loss – but said OK just to keep them happy. So they prayed, and that I thought was the end of that. But a few days later I was alone in the house (everyone else had gone shopping) and suddenly I sensed that God was saying to me, 'You are my son, I am well pleased with you.' I had a real sense that he was my loving heavenly Father, which I had never felt before although I knew in my head that he was.

The other sin on Paul's list that people today would question was the issue of homosexuality. I believe that in the culture of the day sexual appetites were to be indulged, and for many people marriage did not mean abstinence from other sexual liaisons with either sex. Such indulgence of the 'cravings of the heart' is hateful to God; and the Old Testament also forbade men lying with other men as they would with a woman, or dressing in women's clothes – I guess that was based on the principle that we need to accept ourselves as God has made us and not wish to be something else (apart from what God will make us in the new creation!), and that faithfulness in our relationships is part of what it means to be a human made in God's image. What would Paul say to those in our Western culture who live in a faithful, loving, same-sex relationship?

ROMANS CHAPTER 2

[1]Therefore you have nothing to say in your own defence, whoever you are who set yourself up as a judge. In judging others you condemn yourself, for you who set yourself up as a judge do the very same things. [2]And we know that God's judgement falls unerringly on those who do them. [3]You who judge those that do such things and yet are yourself guilty of them – do you suppose that you of all people will escape God's judgement? [4]Or do you think lightly of his abundant kindness, patience, and forbearance, not realising that his kindness is meant to lead you to repentance? [5]Hard-hearted and impenitent as you are, you are storing up for yourself wrath on the day of wrath, when God's justice as a judge will be revealed; [6]for he will give to everyone what their actions deserve. [7]To those who, by perseverance in doing good, aim at glory, honour, and all that is imperishable, he will give immortal life; [8]while as to those who are factious, and disobedient to truth but obedient to evil, wrath and anger, distress and despair, [9]will fall on every human being who persists in wrongdoing – on the Jew

first, but also on the Greek. [10]But there will be glory, honour, and peace for everyone who does right – for the Jew first, but also for the Greek, [11]since God shows no partiality.

When I read a list of sins such as we've just seen in chapter 1, I am tempted to think of those who are guilty of one or more of them and condemn them. But Paul says, in effect, that when you point a finger at someone three fingers are pointing back at yourself. He does not mean that if you condemn someone who is a murderer, that makes you a murderer. He is thinking of what is going on in our hearts. Those who give way to their own cravings and commit heinous sins are in the same spectrum as those of us who give way to our own cravings in small ways. We justify ourselves – 'I'm not doing anyone any harm'. But all of us will have to give an account of our actions on the 'day of wrath' (v. 5), when Jesus returns to earth to judge the living and the dead and to give to everyone what their actions deserve.

I find this teaching quite comforting! There is so much injustice in the world; so many people seem to get away with the most awful crimes, and others suffer wrongly. When Jesus returns to earth he will put everything to rights; that's good news!

This 'day of wrath' is so called because that is the time God's wrath acts against all evil. All evil will be punished. Everyone will have to pay the full price for their evil words and deeds and secret thoughts, unless justice has already been done. (Paul will talk about what Jesus has done for us later in his letter.) God will show no partiality to his own people. However, until that day of wrath, we have time to repent and to align ourselves with the way of life God wants us to live. Those who live the way God wants them to will be judged righteous.

^{12}All who, when they sin, are without Law will also perish without Law; while all who, when they sin, are under Law, will be judged as being under Law. ^{13}It is not those who hear the words of a Law that are righteous before God, but it is those who obey it that will be pronounced righteous. ^{14}When Gentiles, who have no Law, do instinctively what the Law requires, they, though they have no Law, are a Law to themselves; ^{15}for they show the demands of the Law written on their hearts; their consciences corroborating it, while in their thoughts they argue either in self-accusation or, it may be, in self-defence – ^{16}on the day when God passes judgement on people's inmost lives, as the good news that I tell declares that he will do through Christ Jesus.

AT FIRST BLUSH, THIS sounds like a contradiction to what Paul has already written, that God saves everyone who believes, and that the righteousness of God comes by faith. Isn't he saying in these verses that righteousness comes by doing right? In a sense, yes. If someone's life is perfect, and they have done nothing wrong, they are righteous and God will recognise that – he will give to everyone what they deserve, without partiality. The good news of salvation is for those who recognise that they have not done everything right, that they have sinned (the word 'sin' means 'missing the mark'), and deserve God's wrath. A lawyer asked Jesus what he had to do to gain eternal life. Jesus asked him what he thought the Scriptures said. The lawyer answered, love God and your neighbour. Jesus replied, "You are right. Do that, and you will live" (Luke 10:28). Doing right all the time will guarantee a person eternal life.

The Jews were very proud of their godly inheritance – they had been given God's laws about how to worship him, how to behave, and how to conduct their national life. Those without the Jewish law, who didn't know what God's standards were, nevertheless had a sense of right and wrong, and could have a good or bad conscience about their activities. It is not what we know but how we live that matters. But who does right all the time? Who truly measures up to God's standards in the way Jesus taught?

¹⁷But, perhaps, you bear the name of "Jew," and are relying on Law, and boast of belonging to God, and understand his will, ¹⁸and, having been carefully instructed from the Law, have learned to appreciate the finer moral distinctions. ¹⁹Perhaps you are confident that you are a guide to the blind, a light to those who are in the dark, an instructor of the unintelligent, ²⁰and a teacher of the childish, because in the Law you possess the outline of all knowledge and truth. ²¹Why, then, you teacher of others, don't you teach yourself? Do you preach against stealing, and yet steal? ²²Do you forbid adultery, and yet commit adultery? Do you loathe idols,

and yet plunder temples? [23]Boasting, as you do, of your Law, do you dishonour God by breaking the Law?

[24]For, as scripture says – "The Gentiles insult God's name because of you"!

PAUL IS LABOURING THE point, especially to the Jewish Christians in Rome. Before his conversion on the Damascus road he felt that he measured up to God's standards, as he interpreted them in the Scriptures. He had been taught to obey all the Jewish rules and regulations, and he prided himself in being a member of God's special people, the Jews. He had studied under one of the famous Jewish teachers of his day, and no doubt thought that he was indeed 'a guide to the blind, a light to those who are in the dark, an instructor of the unintelligent, and a teacher of the childish'.

Paul's description of their breaches of the law sounds very serious. It may be that he knows of examples of such disobedience – he certainly knows their behaviour had a bad press. (How often do the actions of church members today give Christianity a bad name?) But it may equally be that in the days before his conversion he was tempted to do such things. He was a Pharisee, a member of the strictest sect of Judaism, whose members were thought by the rest of the Jews to be as holy as could be; but Jesus reserved his strongest criticisms for the Pharisees, whom he accused of being hypocrites, not practising what they preached. But even those who did not do such things as Paul describes did not keep the whole law.

^{25}Circumcision has its value, if you are obeying the Law. But, if you are a breaker of the Law, your circumcision is no better than uncircumcision. ^{26}If, then, an uncircumcised man pays regard to the requirements of the Law, won't he, although not circumcised, be regarded by God as if he were? ^{27}Indeed, the person who, owing to his birth, remains uncircumcised, and yet scrupulously obeys the Law, will condemn you, who, for all your written Law and your circumcision, are yet a breaker of the Law. ^{28}For a man who is only a Jew outwardly is not a real Jew; nor is outward bodily circumcision real circumcision. The real Jew is the person who is a Jew in soul; ^{29}and the real circumcision is the circumcision of the heart, a spiritual and not a literal thing. Such a person wins praise from God, though not from people.

THE JEWS WERE DESCENDED from Abraham, and God had promised to be God to him and to his descendants after him. Their relationship to God was marked by male circumcision. However, Paul now knows that those who are truly God's people are those who have a 'circumcision of the heart', when their ungodly self-life is replaced by the new life Christ brings. (He explains about this later.) Physical circumcision only has value when it is accompanied by obedience to all God's commands – but how many Jews could claim they never broke any of God's laws? Who of us can claim to love the Lord our God with all our heart and soul and strength? Yet that is the law (see Deuteronomy 6:5).

Why is Paul saying all this to the Christians in Rome – all of whom he says were dear to God and called to become Christ's people (Romans 1:7)? It may be because he could not be sure that all who would read the letter were genuine believers in Jesus, so he is covering the basics. But I think it more likely that he is concerned for everyone to know the seriousness of their own sin in the light of the coming judgement of God, and to know how important it is to be truly righteous in God's sight. There is no place for any imperfection in the presence of God, and on the day of judgement God will sort out those who are truly righteous from those who are not. (Jesus talks about this in his parable of the sheep and the goats, Matthew 25:31-46.) Those who are not will inevitably be excluded from his presence, and from the amazing new world to come – that's how serious sin is. The good news of salvation tells how God rescues people from judgement and condemnation through Jesus Christ, and how we can become 'a real Jew'. Paul will explain it in the next chapter; but unless we know the danger we humans are in because of our sin, we won't feel the need for salvation either for ourselves or for others.

ROMANS CHAPTER 3

[1]What is the advantage, then, of being a Jew? Or what is the good of circumcision? [2]Great in every way. First of all, because the Jews were entrusted with God's utterances. [3]What follows then? Some, no doubt, showed a want of faith; but will their want of faith make God break faith? Heaven forbid! [4]God must prove true, though everyone prove a liar! As scripture says of God – "That you may be pronounced righteous in what you say, and gain your cause when people would judge you."

If being a Jew, one of God's chosen people, is a matter of a spiritual relationship with God rather than physical ceremonies such as circumcision, then what is the point of circumcision, and do those who are Jews by nature have anything special about them? Paul says Yes, because it was through that natural family, the children of Israel, Abraham's grandson (also known as Jacob), that God revealed himself and his ways to the world. The fact that a relationship with God is primarily a spiritual one does not alter history. God chose the Jews, and they are still his chosen people, as Paul will make clear in chapters 9-11. The history of the Jews is remarkable: since the fall of Jerusalem in AD 70, the loss of their homeland and their scattering across the world, they have survived as a race and kept their traditions and the Scriptures – they are still a people. The history of persecution, especially by Christians who should have honoured them, is a stain upon the human race that we who are not Jews should be deeply ashamed of.

The children of Israel were chosen by God for a purpose: to receive his revelation of himself and his ways so that they would show the world how to live in relationship with the one true God. God had promised their ancestors – especially Abraham – that he would make them a blessing. But they had not fulfilled their task, and often became unfaithful to him, and often anything but a blessing. They broke the covenant relationship they had with God – the covenant summed up in God's words, 'I will be your God, you shall be my people' (Jeremiah 7:23, World English Bible). Did that mean that God had the right to break his side of the bargain? No: God is faithful, he always keeps his promises, and the descendants of Israel are still his chosen people. They have great advantages, says Paul; but that does not protect them from the consequences of their sins. Chosen people or not, they still need salvation!

God is holy; he will always do the right thing. Even when it looks as if God is not keeping his promises (for instance, when he does not seem to have paid any attention to our prayers for peace), the time will come when we will see that is not the case. We may be unfaithful to our promises, for instance when we say we will do something and don't do it (that proves us a liar, v.4); but God will never be unfaithful.

This calls for trust. There will be times when I don't understand how God can possibly claim to be keeping his promises; but I must trust that is because I don't see the whole picture, not because God is breaking his promises. When looking back I can sometimes see that the way things turned out vindicates God, and that he has kept his promises in ways I did not anticipate. This is surely the case with all God's promises about sending a Messiah, a descendant of David; these were fulfilled in Jesus, but not until several hundreds of years had passed, and when they were fulfilled most people did not recognise it. Who could anticipate that the Messiah would be a carpenter from Nazareth? Yet through him immeasurable blessing has come, and God's promises to Abraham and to David have been fulfilled.

[5]But what if our wrongdoing makes God's righteousness all the clearer? Will God be wrong in inflicting punishment? (I can but speak as a person.) Heaven forbid! [6]Otherwise how can God judge the world?

[7]But, if my falsehood redounds to the glory of God, by making his truthfulness more apparent, why am I like others, still condemned as a sinner? [8]Why should we not say – as some people slanderously assert that we do say – "Let us do evil that good may come"? The condemnation of such people is indeed just!

SINFUL ACTIONS MAY have good effects, but that doesn't excuse them. Lights seem to shine brighter in the dark, and the contrast between evil and good shows up the beauty of the good, but that does not justify darkness and evil, and God is right to punish evil however good the outcome of the evil may be. Yet people still accused Paul and his fellow Christians of saying that it is right to do evil so that God's goodness may shine brighter. Why might they say that? Possibly because Christians believed that God had forgiven them and counted them as truly righteous, however wicked they had been; and they assumed that meant Christians could happily go on sinning without fear of punishment. Jews especially would find that thought abhorrent, as they were doing their best not to sin against God. Paul is about to explain in detail what Christians believed, and how that affected their lifestyles, and I think that here he is stating the charge against Christianity before he gives his defence.

I'm afraid I have often found that testimonies from people who have lived wicked lives and then turned to Christ seem much more exciting than testimonies from those who have been brought up in Christian homes; and sometimes I've rather envied those with exciting testimonies – it really shows what God can do. After all, didn't Jesus say there is more joy in heaven over one sinner who repents than over 99 righteous people who do not need to repent? Yet the joy is not for the sin but for the repentance. In John's first letter we read that if we confess our sins, God is faithful and just and will forgive us our sins and purify us from all unrighteousness; but far from putting up with sin, he goes on to say, 'I write this to you so that you will not sin'. Sin is hateful to God; if we have seen his grace and follow Jesus we cannot deliberately choose to do what he hates.

⁹What follows, then? Are we Jews in any way superior to others? Not at all. Our indictment against both Jews and Greeks was that all alike were in subjection to sin.

¹⁰As scripture says –

"There is not even one who is righteous, [11]not one who understands, not one who is searching for God! [12]They have all gone astray; they have one and all become depraved; there is no one who is doing good – no, not one!"

[13]"Their throats are like opened graves; they deceive with their tongues."

"The venom of snakes lies behind their lips,"

[14]"And their mouths are full of bitter curses."

[15]"Swift are their feet to shed blood. [16]Distress and trouble dog their steps, [17]and the path of peace they do not know."

[18]"The fear of God is not before their eyes."

[19]Now we know that everything said in the Law is addressed to those who are under its authority, in order that every mouth may be closed, and to bring the whole world under God's judgement. [20]For no human being will be pronounced righteous before God as the result of obedience to Law; for it is Law that shows what sin is.

THIS IS THE CONCLUSION of the first part of Paul's message to the Romans. Jews need to be saved just as much as non-Jews. Paul quotes several scriptures about sinful behaviour and the lack of righteousness, and points out that those scriptures are written for Jews and need to be taken to heart by them. This is as true today as it was then. We all, Jew or Gentile, Israeli or Palestinian, Christian or Muslim, Buddhist or Hindu, atheist or agnostic, need to be saved from sin and the wrath of God.

I look at those Scriptures and think, 'I'm not like that!' I don't think he is accusing everyone of all that behaviour, but shining a light on humanity as a whole. It balances the common belief that humans are basically good: we are made in God's good image so there is some goodness in everyone, but everyone is also flawed to a greater or lesser extent. None of us is perfect, and that is not an excuse for our wrong-doing! None of us is fit to stand in God's presence, and his laws written in Scripture simply show that up – none of us keeps them perfectly.

This is a difficult pill for most of us to swallow. We live in a world where self-esteem is promoted as most desirable, even essential, and to be told we have all gone astray, that none of us does good, does not go down well. Self-esteem is not bad when it is a reflection of God's esteem of us; he thought it worthwhile to send his only Son to die for us so that we might live with him for ever. (He tells us to love our neighbours as ourselves – self-esteem needs to be matched by esteem for others.) Yet it is just a matter of fact that none of us truly qualifies for the adjective 'good'. Jesus himself told a certain rich ruler who wanted eternal life, "Why do you call me good? No one is good – except God alone." That's the standard goodness is measured by, and our lives so far do not come close. We all miss the mark – we all sin. 'If we say, we have no sin, then we are deceiving ourselves, and the truth is not in us' (1 John 1:8).

Paul is not writing this to make us feel bad – the whole point of the gospel is to give us joy and peace. However, joy and peace cannot be attained by our own efforts and good deeds, even when we feel good about them; it all comes from God, through Jesus. And that is what Paul now goes on to explain. But am I thoroughly convinced that my own goodness – including my faith and good deeds flowing from that faith – is not what qualifies me to inherit eternal life? Not even a tiny little bit? Let me keep my eyes fixed on Jesus!

[21]But now, quite apart from Law, the divine righteousness stands revealed, and to it the Law and the prophets bear witness – [22]the divine righteousness which is bestowed, through faith in Jesus Christ, on all, without distinction, who believe in him. [23]For all have sinned, and all fall short of God's glorious ideal, [24]but, in his loving kindness, are being freely pronounced righteous through the deliverance found in Christ Jesus. [25]For God set him before the world, to be, by the shedding of his blood, a means of reconciliation through faith. And this God did to prove his righteousness, and because, in his forbearance, he had passed over the sins that people had previously committed; [26]as a proof, I repeat, at the present time, of his own righteousness, that he might be righteous in our eyes, and might pronounce righteous the person who takes their stand on faith in Jesus.

HOW CAN WE BE RIGHTEOUS and acceptable in the sight of our holy God? Not by our obedience, for as we have seen, our obedience is too imperfect. The word 'righteous' describes God – it is what God is. Anything less than God's righteousness is not true righteousness. Righteousness is not just about doing the right thing; it is primarily about relationships, as we saw in chapter 1:17. God's righteousness describes how God relates to his creatures, especially to human beings who are made in his image and are able to relate to him. God's love for us, his care for us, the way he keeps his promises to us, all these are facets of his righteousness just as much as the way he always does what is good and right. Now, says Paul, that righteousness has been revealed through Jesus and his sacrifice for us, as the Jewish Scriptures foretold. It has not come out of the blue. It is not at all contrary to Scripture, although it is 'quite apart from the Law' – it is not just a matter of obeying God's commands, thankfully!

What makes us righteous in God's eyes is faith in Jesus the Messiah ('Christ'), who was sent by God to save the world. We put our trust in him as our own living lord and saviour, and trust him to look after us and lead us into eternal life with God. When we do that God forgives us all our sins and declares us righteous, bringing us into a close and loving relationship with him. Paul makes clear that this righteousness is a gift which God bestows on all who believe in Jesus, without distinction. Jew or Gentile, slave or free, male or female, rich or poor, however good or bad we have been, all are offered this gift. We all have sinned, and fallen short of the glory of God – both 'God's glorious ideal' and the glorious future God has planned for us with him – so our righteousness is not a product of our own efforts or life-style or nationality or family history. It only comes through faith in the 'deliverance found in Christ Jesus' who gave his life as a sacrifice for us that we might be forgiven and delivered from God's wrath, set free to live with God.

Jesus' sacrifice, and the reconciliation with God that it brings, was a public display (v. 25). God wants everyone to see it, so that they may believe and be reconciled to him. He wants everyone to see that it displays both his love and his righteousness in dealing fully with their sin. A good and holy God cannot leave sins unpunished, however much he loves the sinner; yet he was known as a God of mercy who forgave sin and counted people as righteous throughout Biblical history. How could a righteous God simply overlook sin? The cross of Jesus is the answer – Jesus bore our sins on the cross. He suffered the full penalty for sin, on our behalf. Jesus' death was a sacrifice of reconciliation for all of time, BC (BCE) as well as AD (CE). Thus God shows himself to be righteous, while being able to pronounce each one of us as righteous, whoever 'takes their stand on faith in Jesus.' I cannot take my stand on how well I have lived my life. I have fallen short! Righteousness is a sheer gift – I have not earned it, I do not deserve it. And this gift is offered to all. Good news indeed! What a gift! What love! Oh that the world might taste and see!

What about those who have never heard the good news? Many people ask that question, and I don't know the answer fully. I know they need to hear, so that they can have the opportunity to live confidently with God in faith and know his promise of eternal life through Jesus. I suspect many are in the same situation as all those who lived before Jesus was born, many of whom were people of faith in God's salvation, as Hebrews 11 makes clear. God knows their hearts, and loves them far more than we ever could; so I am sure he will treat them with infinite love and justice. But that doesn't relieve us of our responsibility to share the good news.

²⁷What, then, becomes of our boasting? It is excluded. By what sort of Law? A Law requiring obedience? No, a Law requiring faith.

²⁸For we conclude that a person is pronounced righteous on the ground of faith, quite apart from obedience to Law. ²⁹Or can it be that God is the God only of the Jews? Isn't he also the God of the Gentiles?

³⁰Yes, of the Gentiles also, since there is only one God, and he will pronounce those who are circumcised righteous as the result of faith, and also those who are uncircumcised on their showing the same faith.

³¹Do we, then, use this faith to abolish Law? Heaven forbid! No, we establish Law.

PAUL NOW LOOKS DEEPER into the issues of faith and obedience – in particular, the issues relevant to the people to whom he is writing. He himself had once prided himself on his Jewish heritage and on his obedience to God's revealed law (Philippians 3:4ff); now he recognises that such pride was ill-founded, for our relationship with God is not something we can inherit, nor achieve by our own work or merit. We have nothing to boast about. Jesus has opened the gate of eternal life for us, and knowing and following him in faith is all that matters. God is God not just of those who know the Law, but of everyone in the world; and a loving relationship with him is for all who believe in Jesus whether or not they have been circumcised in obedience to the Law.

Does that mean that the Law is abolished? That was a very relevant question for Paul's readers - especially the Jewish believers. No, says Paul, Heaven forbid! (literally, 'May it not be'!) Paul valued the Law; Jesus had said, "Not even the smallest letter, nor one stroke of a letter, will disappear from the Law until all is done" (Matthew 5:18). However, the Law was not the way to God; that way is through faith in Jesus. Faith does not replace law, but fulfils it; true obedience to God is not something that the written law can produce, but springs from faith, as James also makes clear in his letter (James 2:14-26).

If obedience to God's law – 'doing the right thing' – is not the way to eternal life with God, what is the place of the Old Testament law for me today? The Law and the Prophets were inspired by God (2 Timothy 3:16), and will only disappear when all is accomplished – indeed, faith establishes it (v. 31); so what is it for nowadays? I believe the law is still God's word, and different parts of the law and the prophets have different functions. Some of it reveals how God wants human beings to live – without theft, murder, adultery etc. Some of it reveals how God wanted his people to live in the land he gave them – instructions about agriculture, government, buildings etc. Some of it reveals how God wanted people to worship him in the days before the Messiah came – much of which pointed forward to the work of Christ and helps us understand his work more fully. The stories in the Old Testament reveal human failings as well as human faithfulness. All of it reveals the nature and character of God. That's why it is still part of the Christian Bible! When I read it in the light of the New Testament, knowing that the God of the Old Testament is the God and Father of our Lord Jesus Christ who fully reveals God's character, then I get to know God better. Yes, I find parts are very difficult and hard to swallow. But the more I read the more I understand. I still have a number of questions, but one day 'I will know in full, as I have been fully known.'

ROMANS CHAPTER 4

[1]What then, it may be asked, are we to say about Abraham, the ancestor of our nation? [2]If he was pronounced righteous as the result of obedience, then he has something to boast of. Yes, but not before God.

[3]For what are the words of scripture? "Abraham had faith in God, and his faith was regarded by God as righteousness." [4]Now wages are regarded as due to the person who works, not as a favour, but as a debt; [5]while, as for the person who does not rely on their obedience, but has faith in him who can pronounce the godless righteous, their faith is regarded by God as righteousness.

[6]In precisely the same way David speaks of the blessing pronounced on the person who is regarded by God as righteous apart from actions – [7]"Blessed are those whose wrongdoings have been forgiven and over whose sins a veil has been drawn! [8]Blessed the man whom the Lord will never regard as sinful!"

Paul has stated that God sees us as righteous on account of our faith in Jesus the Messiah, not on account of our merit or ancestry. This would have raised a question in the minds of his Jewish readers, for they had been brought up to see themselves as descendants of Abraham through Isaac and Jacob (Israel), and beneficiaries of God's promises to Abraham – especially Genesis 17:7: 'I will establish my covenant between me and you and your offspring after you throughout their generations for an everlasting covenant, to be a God to you and to your offspring after you.' When God said that, he went on to tell Abram (his name at that time) that he, his household and all his male descendants had to be circumcised as a sign of that covenant – it was a 'covenant in their flesh'. Paul knew and accepted all this. He also knew that in the next chapter of Genesis God told Abraham that he had chosen him "to the end that he may command his children and his household after him, that they may keep the way of Yahweh, to do righteousness and justice; to the end that Yahweh may bring on Abraham that which he has spoken of him" ('Yahweh' is the name of God, in many versions written as LORD to avoid misuse). The covenant only applied to those who did what was right and just – those who were obedient to God. That was the foundation of the Jewish religion. But Paul also knew that sometime before all this God had told the childless Abram, 'Look now toward the sky, and count the stars, if you are able to count them. So will your offspring be.' Abram believed the Lord, and 'his faith was regarded by God as righteousness' (Genesis 15:6). It is this statement that Paul uses to underline his message to the Jewish Christians in Rome.

First, he notes that God credited Abram with righteousness simply because Abram believed his promise. Usually we reckon someone as righteous because their lives show they merit it – they are good people. That is not the case here. It was not Abram's obedience that merited his standing before God, but his faith. Then Paul quotes Psalm 32:1-2, written by King David a thousand years later. David certainly knew he was guilty of sins, yet he believed God could – and did in his own case – draw a veil over a person's sin and regard them as righteous. Thus Paul shows that true righteousness is a gift from God, not something merited or deserved.

I know this is true. Yet I too often feel sinful and under condemnation, rather than righteous because of God's amazing gift. Paul needs to drive home this lesson to me, as well as to his first readers!

⁹Is this blessing, then, pronounced on the circumcised only or on the uncircumcised as well? We say that – "Abraham's faith was regarded by God as righteousness."

¹⁰Under what circumstances, then, did this take place? After his circumcision or before it? ¹¹Not after, but before. And it was as a sign of this that he received the rite of circumcision – to show the righteousness due to the faith of an uncircumcised man – in order that he might be the father of all who have faith in God even when uncircumcised, so that they also may be regarded by God as righteous; ¹²as well as father of the circumcised – to those who are not only circumcised, but who also follow our father Abraham in that faith which he had while still uncircumcised. ¹³For the

promise that he should inherit the world did not come to Abraham or his descendants through Law, but through the righteousness due to faith. [14]If those who take their stand on Law are to inherit the world, then faith is robbed of its meaning and the promise comes to nothing!

PAUL NOW RETURNS TO the Scripture he quoted in v. 3 of this chapter. He points out that God counted Abraham as righteous long before his circumcision; and he draws the conclusion that circumcision was a sign and a seal of Abraham's faith. Righteousness was God's gift to a man of faith, before there was any law or regulation to obey; so Abraham is the spiritual father of all who have faith, whether or not they are circumcised. Likewise God had promised Abram in Genesis 12 that he would be a blessing to many nations – which Paul interprets as 'he should inherit the world' – and again, this promise was made at the beginning of Abram's story, long before he was circumcised. Paul makes the point that such promises were worthless if they depended on people obeying the law; they were unconditional promises, made to a person who through faith was accepted by God as righteous.

Is this just an academic argument? Is Paul simply scoring points? I don't think so. I think this is a vitally important part of his teaching, for Abraham was the founder of his faith and ours. God had chosen one man in the whole world to be the beginning of his good news of salvation for the world – through him and his offspring the whole world would be blessed. All that was required of him was to trust and obey. His story is not heroic – he did many wrong things in my view – but God's covenant with him to be his God, and for him and his descendants to be God's people, is the basis of the whole Bible. Abraham's response of faith, and God's counting that faith as the righteousness required for a close relationship with him, sets the course for all his descendants, whether physical or spiritual.

¹⁵Law entails punishment; but, where no Law exists, no breach of it is possible. ¹⁶That is why everything is made to depend on faith: so that everything may be God's gift, and in order that the fulfilment of the promise may be made certain for all Abraham's descendants – not only for those who take their stand on the Law, but also for those who take their stand on the faith of Abraham. (He is the father of us all; ¹⁷as scripture says – "I have made you the father of many nations.") And this they do in the sight of that God in whom Abraham had faith, and who gives life to the dead, and speaks of what does not yet exist as if it did.

ONE IMPORTANT ASPECT of the rule of law is that it has to be enforced by punishing those who break the law. However, it cannot be enforced upon those who live outside its jurisdiction – before circumcision was commanded, there was nothing wrong with being uncircumcised. But when righteousness depends on faith rather than obedience, that takes away the need to enforce a law – righteousness is a gift of God, received by faith, available to all whether or not they are under the law God has revealed. Those who, like Abraham, believe God's promises, are counted as

Abraham's spiritual descendants whatever their ethnic or cultural background; and they inherit the promises given to Abraham and his descendants. A faith like Abraham's takes no account of how possible or impossible a promise's fulfilment seems; and that faith is seen and recognised by God.

[18]With no ground for hope, Abraham, sustained by hope, put faith in God; in order that, in fulfilment of the words – "So many will your descendants be," he might become "the father of many nations." [19]Though he was nearly a hundred years old, yet his faith did not fail him, even when he thought of his own body, then utterly worn out, and remembered that Sarah was past bearing children. [20]He was not led by want of faith to doubt God's promise. [21]On the contrary, his faith gave him strength; and he praised God, in the firm conviction that what God has promised he is also able to carry out. [22]And therefore his faith "was regarded as righteousness." [23]Now these words – "it was regarded as righteousness" – were not written with reference to Abraham only; [24]but also with reference to us. Our faith, too, will be regarded by God in the same light, if we have faith in him who raised Jesus, our Lord, from the dead; [25]for Jesus was given up to death to atone for our offences, and was raised to life that we might be pronounced righteous.

WHAT EXACTLY IS A FAITH like Abraham's? It is a faith that has a 'firm conviction that what God has promised he is also able to carry out'. Abraham trusted God even though, as a childless old man, it seemed impossible for him to have descendants. When God regarded his faith as righteous he was already fairly old (over 75, according to the Bible – though there is some debate about how years were reckoned in those days). Later he was persuaded by his wife to attempt to fulfil God's promise by taking her servant girl as his wife; the girl did indeed have a son, but that was not the son God had planned. Childless Sarah would be the mother, and her having a son was certainly a miracle, a gift of God who through their faith gave Abraham and Sarah the ability to have a child in the normal way. That is the sort of faith that God regards as righteous – and God regards us as righteous too when we have that sort of a faith in a God who can 'do the impossible' by raising Jesus to life from the dead.

I find that my faith in God's promise to do something increases when I can see how it might be possible. That is not a faith like Abraham's. He believed God simply because he trusted him - his faith was based on God's nature and character, not on possibilities – no task is impossible for God. I must learn to look at God more than the apparent circumstances – especially when praying for people or situations.

The mention of Jesus' death and resurrection brings Paul back to speak of the righteousness we have through Jesus. True righteousness, which brings us into a close relationship with God, requires that all our offences and shortcomings be forgiven and that God himself accepts us and regards us as if our lives were good and perfect. That is the righteousness we are given when we believe in Jesus. He was put to death for our offences, to bear the punishment they deserve; his death wiped them out, and they no longer count against us. Some people don't think that's fair: why should Jesus suffer for the wrong I have done? They are right – it is not fair. It is grace. Jesus, in love for us, took us as his people and willingly took responsibility for all we have done. God raised him to life for us because justice had been done and all our sins were atoned for; now Jesus – and we – can live for ever in the presence of God. His perfect life is counted as ours, and we too are pronounced righteous and accepted by God.

How does this work? 'Taking responsibility for all we have done' is not the whole picture. In this letter Paul talks a lot about us being 'in' Christ, receiving God's grace and gifts 'through Christ'. This points to something that he will speak about in more detail in Chapter 6: when we believe in Jesus we are united to him, not physically but spiritually. He takes responsibility for us because we are united to him; and his perfect life is counted as ours because that's what it is – his resurrection life is flowing through us, his life is united to ours. Theologians call this our 'mystical union', and it is very mystical! But it's true! Our natural life will come to an end; but the life we have in union with Christ will never end. We have glorious hope!

I am reminded of several verses of the Bible from Paul's second letter to the Corinthians:

'God, in Christ, was reconciling the world to himself, not reckoning people's offences against them' (2 Corinthians 5:19).

'For our sake God made Christ, who was innocent of sin, one with our sinfulness, so that in him we might be made one with the righteousness of God' (2 Corinthians 5:21).

'For you do not forget the loving kindness of our Lord Jesus Christ – how that for your sakes, although he was rich, he became poor, so that you also might become rich through his poverty' (2 Corinthians 8:9).

Lord, may I see these truths in all their grace and glory!

ROMANS CHAPTER 5

¹Therefore, having been pronounced righteous as the result of faith, let us enjoy peace with God through Jesus Christ, our Lord. ²It is through him that, by reason of our faith, we have obtained admission to that place in God's favour in which we now stand. So let us exult in our hope of attaining God's glorious ideal.

We who believe in Jesus have been pronounced righteous – God the ultimate judge declares we are innocent of all wrong-doing; he has nothing against us. We are united to Jesus, and Jesus is completely free from every stain of sin, even though he took the blame for the whole world. He bore our sins on the cross, and paid the full penalty for every one. Jesus, as a resurrected human being who has ascended into heaven, is now right beside God, in the closest possible relationship with him. And that's our position too, for we are spiritually one with him. We have complete peace with God, the same sort of peace that Jesus has with his Father.

I am aware that some folk don't want peace with God, because they think that if God exists he is responsible for the mess this world is in: either he is powerless to do anything about it (he is not almighty), or doesn't want to (he is not loving). My own belief is that God certainly could end the mess if he wanted to – that will happen on judgement day – but that he doesn't want to end it yet, because he has something better in mind. What that 'better' is, is open to question; I think it is partly his desire to give people time to change their minds about him before having to give an account of themselves, but also maybe because he needs to conquer all evil, and that involves giving time for evil to be seen for what it is.

Jesus told a story about wheat and weeds – weeds which in their early stages probably were difficult to distinguish from wheat. The weeds had been sown among the wheat by an enemy. The servants asked if they should root them out, but the farmer told them to wait until harvest, for it would be impossible to root out the weeds without rooting out some wheat as well. I believe that when God allows evil to happen, it is for his loving purposes – I am prepared to trust his power and love and wisdom even when I don't understand why he acts as he does. Peace with God depends on faith in his nature and character; and if we believe what Jesus shows and teaches us about that, then peace with God is most desirable.

The translation we are using says 'let us enjoy peace with God', whereas most other translations say 'we have peace with God'; both translations are equally good, so it all depends on what we think Paul is trying to get across. Personally, I feel that Paul is getting across truths that are such good news that joy should be the natural response! The righteousness we now have through Christ means we are at peace with God and in good favour with him, and that is a matter for joy: moreover, through Jesus we too have the hope of experiencing the glory of God – that, too, is something to rejoice in. Jesus is in glory now; Paul will tell us in chapter 8 that we are children of God, and co-heirs with Christ, 'since we share Christ's sufferings in order that we may also share his glory' (Romans 8:17).

Paul is going to talk about suffering next. However, this talk of exulting in our present position reminds me that we are incredibly blessed – more blessed than anyone who has won a lottery! 'Joyless Christians' is a contradiction – how can we be joyless when God has done so much for us and has so much in store for us? That's not to say that Christians should never be depressed or in despair – Paul experienced despair at times (2 Corinthians 1:8), and depression can't simply be argued away. Nevertheless, our feelings cannot mask the fact of our peace with God and our hope of glory hereafter. We can have peace with God even in the darkness.

³And not only that, but let us also exult in our troubles;

⁴for we know that trouble develops endurance, and endurance strength of character, and strength of character hope...

HOW ON EARTH CAN PAUL exult in troubles, and expect us to do the same? I'm sure he wasn't happy and glad about the suffering his troubles caused him. How can Christians in northern Nigeria rejoice and be glad when Boko Haram come, killing villagers and abducting children, looting and destroying homes and churches? Yet in the sermon on the mount Jesus said that when persecuted, 'Be glad and rejoice, because your reward in heaven will be great; this is the way they persecuted the prophets who lived before you.' I notice that Jesus doesn't tell Christians under persecution to be happy about the suffering they are experiencing, but to be happy about the great reward they will receive. And Paul told the Corinthians, 'Though outwardly we are wasting away, yet inwardly we are being renewed day by day. The light burden of our momentary trouble is preparing for us a weight of imperishable glory, beyond all measure' (2 Corinthians 4:16-17). If I am vaccinated against 'flu or Covid, that procedure may hurt a bit; but if it brings protection against a serious infection I can be glad I've had it.

Paul speaks here about one way troubles can benefit us. Trouble develops endurance which develops character which develops hope. I don't think this is always all or nothing: we don't have to endure everything to the bitter end in order to fully develop endurance, character and hope. When our family was caught in a civil war in Uganda we stayed where we were for quite a time; but there came a point where we saw it was having an adverse effect on our children, and decided to move. We felt bad about leaving our Ugandan friends and colleagues, who couldn't do the same. Yet what we had endured up to then had its effect, I am sure, and changed us as people and built up our faith.

There may be occasions when we are called to be faithful to Jesus to the end, to keep trusting in his promises and in the goodness of God despite strong temptation to give up our faith. God is gracious, however, and more often helps us to start growing in character through enduring minor troubles before we have to face major ones. And we have this statement in Scripture: 'God will not fail you, and he will not allow you to be tempted beyond your strength; but, when he sends the temptation, he will also provide the way of escape, so that you may have strength to endure' (1 Corinthians 10:13).

...[5]and that hope never disappoints. For the love of God has filled our hearts through the Holy Spirit which was given us; [6]seeing that, while we were still powerless, Christ, in God's good time, died on behalf of the godless. [7]Even for an upright person scarcely anyone will die. For a really good person perhaps someone might even dare to die. [8]But God puts his love for us beyond all doubt by the fact that Christ died on our behalf while we were still sinners. [9]Much more, then, now that we have been pronounced righteous by virtue of the shedding of his blood, will we be saved through him from the wrath of God. [10]For if, when we were God's enemies, we were reconciled to him through the death of his Son, much more, now that we have become reconciled, will we be saved by virtue of Christ's life.

[11]And not only that, but we exult in God, through Jesus Christ, our Lord, through whom we have now obtained this reconciliation.

THE HOPE PAUL IS TALKING about is the hope of sharing the glory of God, 'God's glorious ideal' (v. 2). Strength of character develops hope, he says. I think that underlying this expression is the thought that what we will be in the new creation will reflect what we have become in this world. We are told to press on to maturity in our faith (see Philippians 3:13-15). We know that in the new creation we will be perfect, like Christ; but just as he still has the marks of his crucifixion, so I believe my perfection will include the marks of my earthly life, especially if those marks have helped me to become more gloriously godly. The thought strikes me that God's glory is not so much his power and majesty but his love; what we most look forward to is not so much our future honour and status but our future loving relationship with God.

'That hope never disappoints,' says Paul. It is a certain hope, and the proof of that is the presence of the Holy Spirit in a believer. The Holy Spirit is the Spirit of God, who Christians believe is the third Person of the Holy Trinity, alongside God the Father and God the Son. He (I use the traditional pronoun although I know we cannot assign a gender to the Spirit) is as intimately related to God as my human spirit is related to me; what the Spirit does, God does. And if the Holy Spirit is living in me, then God is living in me – and that proves I am fully acceptable to God.

The Holy Spirit is the one through whom God's love has been 'poured out' (literally) on us – that is the primary reason we know he is living in us. The love that the Spirit pours into our lives is God's love for us, the foundation of our faith and of our life with God. We see that love in Christ's death for us: he died for us while we were unable to make ourselves righteous and were godless sinners (vs. 6, 8), even enemies (v. 10). Paul reflects on the magnitude of love that inspires some people to die for others; but Christ's love is vaster by far. Through his loving death for us we are pronounced righteous here and now so that we can live in the love of God. I think Paul's expression implies he expects us to be fully aware of God's love for us here and now; the Spirit enables us to feel it in our spirits. (I remember gospel tracts which told us that feelings followed faith, which followed facts - we don't expect feelings to come first. We learn the facts about Jesus, enough to put our faith in him; and then we can expect feelings to follow, at least on occasions.) In the future we will have to face judgement and give an account of our lives, but we don't need to be afraid of that – if God lives in us by his Spirit, it is because he has already accepted us, and our safety on the day of judgement is guaranteed. It is all because of Jesus, who has saved us and will save us. 'God was in Christ, reconciling the world to himself' (1 Corinthians 5:19). Christ is now living with God, and we are spiritually united to him, now and for all eternity (provided we don't desert him, John 15:6, 9, 10).

All this is not just the love of Jesus alone. Jesus lived in the love of his Father, and told people he only did what he saw his Father doing. Jesus' love for us exhibits God's love for us, and God is the one who raised Jesus to new life, and through that action raised us to new life also – because he loves us so much. We can truly exult in God's love!

Thinking about this, I am amazed by the immensity of God's love for insignificant little me! If he thus loved me before I really thought about him, how much more, now that my life is hidden with Christ in God (see Colossians 3:2), can I appreciate and enjoy his love! This must be an answer to my prayer at the end of the last chapter: If I want the Lord to 'light the flame within my heart' so that 'I will love thee more and more" (as one old hymn puts it), then surely I need to spend time basking – and exulting – in the love of God for me. As John puts it, 'We love, because God first loved us' (1 John 4:19). "But I don't deserve it," I think. God knows I don't deserve it. And that's the thrust of Paul's argument – we deserve God's love far, far, less than we think or feel, yet he loves us far, far more than we can ever think or feel, and has made it possible to welcome us home with open arms, through Jesus. It really is amazing grace.

[12]Therefore, just as sin came into the world through one man, and through sin came death; so, also, death spread to all humanity, because every person has sinned. [13]Even before the time of the Law there was sin in the world; but sin cannot be charged against someone where no Law exists. [14]Yet, from Adam to Moses, death reigned even over those whose sin was not a breach of a law, as Adam's was. And Adam foreshadows the one to come.

[15]But there is a contrast between Adam's offence and God's gracious gift. For, if by reason of the offence of the one man the whole human race died, far more were the loving kindness of God, and the gift given in the loving kindness of the one man, Jesus Christ, lavished on the whole human race. [16]There is a contrast, too, between the gift and the results of the one man's sin. The judgement, which followed on the one man's sin, resulted in condemnation, but God's gracious gift, which followed on many offences, resulted in a decree of righteousness. [17]For if, by reason of the offence of the one man, death reigned through that one man, far more will those, on whom God's loving kindness and his gift of righteousness are lavished, find life, and reign through the one man, Jesus Christ. [18]Briefly then, just as a single offence resulted for all humanity in condemnation, so, too, a single decree of righteousness resulted for all humanity in that declaration of righteousness which

brings life. [19]For, as through the disobedience of the one man the whole human race was rendered sinful, so, too, through the obedience of the one, the whole human race will be rendered righteous. [20]Law was introduced in order that offences might be multiplied. But, where sins were multiplied, the loving kindness of God was lavished the more, [21]in order that, just as sin had reigned in the realm of death, so, too, might loving-kindness reign through righteousness, and result in eternal life, through Jesus Christ, our Lord.

PAUL SEEMS TO INTRODUCE a new subject here, but he begins with the word 'Therefore', which seems to me to imply that his thought was following on from what he's just said. I think he was going to say, 'Therefore, just as sin came into the world through one man, and through sin came death, so also righteousness and peace with God has come into the world through one man, and through righteousness comes life.' He has talked about Abraham and his descendants; now he widens the picture to include the whole human race descended from Adam. But his thought runs away with him, and he doesn't finish the sentence but gets carried away to talk about sin coming into the world through Adam. (The Hebrew name 'Adam' means 'man'.) Adam disobeyed an explicit command from God, and as the forefather of the human race (whether literally or spiritually is not an issue here), the consequence of his sin affected the whole race just as a head of state's decisions affect a whole nation. The consequence of sin is separation from God, what Paul calls 'death' later on in this letter. That is just the nature of things: if we do not match up to God's righteousness we are not fit for his presence nor for his kingdom, and from Adam onwards all fall short of the glory of God. Yet, as I have said, I believe there is a sense of right and wrong, of what is fair and what is not fair, throughout the human race; and that sense exists whether or not there is a legal system that spells out right and wrong and seeks to enforce the right by punishing wrong-doing.

Paul sees Jesus as a second Adam, another representative of the human race, but this time far better. I don't believe God made a mistake with Adam; he knew beforehand all that was going to happen. Adam would never have sinned if God hadn't given him free choice; but what would human life be like if there was no possibility of making the wrong choice? Anyway, Adam foreshadowed the one to come – a pale shadow! Adam's offence was due to self-interest; the gift of God, his only Son, was due to amazing love. Adam's offence brought condemnation and death to all; Jesus made righteousness and life available to all. The law came in to control human behaviour; but it resulted in greater disobedience. Yet God's grace kept pace with ever greater grace: 'where offences increase, the loving kindness of God was lavished the more.' Evil reigned; looking at the world today we see it still does. But love is stronger, and God's loving kindness will end up reigning through righteousness, bringing eternal life.

This translation says 'the whole human race' in v. 19, whereas the original Greek simply says 'the many'. I don't think Paul means to imply that the whole of the present human race will be made righteous; he is teaching that everyone who is united to Jesus through faith in him is rendered righteous, through Jesus' obedience. Paul here is presenting Jesus as the founder of a new race of human beings. Adam founded the present race of humans; Jesus was the first of a new creation of human beings with new, eternal, life – the kind of human beings that God all along had planned. When we believe in Jesus we are 'born again' into this new life – the germ of new creation has been planted in our old creation bodies, to flourish into its fullness when Jesus returns. He will then bring this old creation to an end and judge the living and the dead, before bringing the new creation to fulfilment. Jesus' resurrection body is the pattern for the bodies we will have after our own resurrection/transformation when Jesus returns. His body now is recognisably human, and recognisably Jesus – it bears the marks of his crucifixion, but it is different from the body he had before he died. It is immortal, he could appear in locked rooms, but Jesus was still the same Jesus. Paul tells the Corinthians that the new body is spiritual, not earthly; I presume the new creation will have different biology, chemistry and physics! Be that as it may, our new bodies will be new creation bodies like that of Jesus after his resurrection; and they, too, will be recognisable, perfect and glorious! Paul goes even further: we not only find life, we 'will reign through the one man, Jesus Christ.' Jesus already has all authority in heaven and on earth (Matthew 28:18), and somehow, in a way we can't imagine yet, we will share that authority!

ROMANS CHAPTER 6

[1]What are we to say, then? Are we to continue to sin, in order that God's loving kindness may be multiplied? [2]Heaven forbid! We became dead to sin, so how can we go on living in it? [3]Or can it be that you do not know that all of us, who were baptised into union with Christ Jesus, in our baptism shared his death? [4]Consequently, through sharing his death in our baptism, we were buried with him; so that, just as Christ was raised from the dead by a manifestation of the Father's power, so we also may live a new life. [5]If we have become united with him by the act symbolic of his death, surely we will also become united with him by the act symbolic of his resurrection. [6]We recognise the truth that our old self was crucified with Christ, in order that the body, the stronghold of sin, might be rendered powerless, so that we should no longer be slaves to sin. [7]For the man who has so died has been pronounced righteous and released from sin. [8]And our belief is, that, as we have shared Christ's death, we will also share his life. [9]We know, indeed, that Christ, having once risen from the dead, will not die again. Death has power over him no

longer. [10]For the death that he died was a death to sin, once and for all. But the life that he now lives, he lives for God. [11]So let it be with you – regard yourselves as dead to sin, but as living for God, through union with Christ Jesus.

Paul's teaching that the law multiplied our offences and that the loving kindness of God was lavished the more, could easily be twisted: if the more we sin, the more God forgives and the greater the glory of his grace, then why not sin the more so that God's glorious grace may increase? Many people would respond, 'Ah, but we should not do that, because it would be against God's will.' While that is true, Paul does not use that argument. He takes the opportunity to teach truths that are fundamental to our lives as Christians.

The most important teaching is that those who believe in Jesus are united to him in a real and transforming way. Baptism is the badge of faith, marking the beginning of the Christian journey. (This is why some branches of Christianity insist that baptism should only be done after a person has come to believe; others believe it is right to baptise believers' children who are being brought up in the Christian faith. Obviously any baptised person can stop following Jesus, whether or not they were baptised as believers.) In Paul's day most Christians came to faith in Jesus as adults, though we do read of whole households being baptised. The point Paul is making is that they were baptised 'into' Christ, into union with him, and that meant they were now united with one who had died. They had been 'born again' into a new kind of life, a life-after-death kind of life, a Jesus kind of life. They had been spiritually transformed, and what happens to us spiritually has an effect on our bodies and minds and emotions.

I find the illustration of a body and its parts quite helpful here – Paul uses that picture later in the letter. Each of us who believe in Jesus are united to him rather like a transplanted organ is united to a receiver's body. Imagine, for instance, that I receive a transplanted hand. My hands are involved in everything that I do, receiving nourishment from the food I eat, commands from my brain, and so forth. I take responsibility for what my hands do; I can't say, "It was not me, it was my hands." In the same way Jesus takes responsibility for all his people do – they are like parts of his body. That's why he died: he was taking responsibility for all our wrong-doing. That's also why he rose again. If an organ is transplanted into us it becomes part of our body and our life flows through it, our life with all its history. If a memory made our old heart beat a little faster, it will make a new heart do the same. And when we believe in Jesus, we become part of a Body that died and was raised to life again, and the results of that death and resurrection now affect us too: our sins are forgiven, and we have Christ's resurrection life flowing through us.

Our baptism into Christ, and all that follows, has a purpose: that we might live a new life, a Christ-like life. The Christ we are now united with is the Jesus who died – and who rose from the dead and is now alive. Both his death and his resurrection are now in our own spiritual histories. As Paul says, we have been crucified with Christ – not physically, obviously, but in a way that is real and transformative. Exactly what has happened to us is a mystery to me, but the consequences are clear. When Jesus died he died a 'death to sin': his body could no longer do anything, and certainly could not sin! Paul regards 'sin' as an active power, enslaving a person so that they cannot live the way God wants, but fall short. A dead person is no longer enslaved; and our union with our crucified Saviour has the effect of freeing us from slavery to sin. We still live in our old-creation bodies, and can still be tempted; but we no longer have to give in to those temptations, and are now able to choose what God wants instead – indeed, we want to live God's way. We are united to Christ's risen life, and he lives for God. If that is the case, how can we possibly want to continue in sin?

Nevertheless, a choice remains. We can choose to believe that we are united with Jesus in his death and resurrection life, or not. Paul urges his readers – including us – to see ourselves in the way that God sees us, as dead to sin and living for God in union with Christ Jesus. This is not imaginative fiction: we are not trying to make ourselves believe something that is not true. Paul is encouraging us to open our eyes and see the truth about ourselves. That is not easy. If a poor person wins, or is given, a huge amount of money, that might be difficult to come to terms with because old habits die hard, and their way of life might be hard to change. Nevertheless, the truth would remain: they are rich. Nicky Gumbel in the 'Alpha Course' tells the story of an old lady to whom exactly that happened: she died in apparent poverty, but was discovered to have inherited great riches. Yet I and so many Christians act in the same way, and do not 'cash in' the spiritual riches we've been given! Lord, open the eyes of our hearts, that we may see and believe the truth about ourselves, that we are indeed dead to sin and living for God through our union with Christ Jesus.

Paul goes on to say more about what that means in practice.

[12]Therefore do not let sin reign in your mortal bodies and compel you to obey its cravings. [13]Do not offer any part of your bodies to sin, in the cause of unrighteousness, but once for all offer yourselves to God (as those who, though once dead, now have life), and devote every part of your bodies to the cause of righteousness. [14]For sin will not lord it over you. You are living under the reign, not of Law, but of love.

[15]What follows, then? Are we to sin because we are living under the reign of love and not of Law? Heaven forbid! [16]Surely you know that when you offer yourselves as servants, to obey anyone, you are the servants of the person whom you obey, whether the service be a service to sin which leads to death, or a service to duty which leads to righteousness. [17]God be thanked that, though you were once servants of sin, yet you learned to give hearty obedience to that form of doctrine under which you were placed. [18]Set free from the control of sin, you became servants to righteousness. [19]I can but speak as people do because of the weakness of your earthly nature. Once you offered every part of your bodies to the service of impurity, and of wickedness, which leads to further wickedness. Now, in the same way, offer them to the service of righteousness, which leads to holiness. [20]While you were still servants of sin, you were free as regards righteousness. [21]But

what were the fruits that you reaped from those things of which you are now ashamed? For the end of such things is death. [22]But now that you have been set free from the control of sin, and have become servants to God, the fruit that you reap is an ever-increasing holiness, and the end eternal life. [23]The wages of sin are death, but the gift of God is eternal life, through union with Christ Jesus, our Lord.

WHEN WE BELIEVE IN Jesus we are given Jesus' resurrection life. However, that life does not extend to our bodies. They will die and we will be resurrected when Jesus returns (or we will be transformed if Jesus returns while we're still alive). While we live in our mortal bodies our brains and feelings and habits continue, so we still have a choice how to live, whether to follow our old way of life or the new. Through our faith we are counted righteous, and are free from the power of sin and are members of the kingdom of God, under his reign of love; but are we free to use our freedom and privileged position to continue doing things God does not want? Of course not, says Paul. The right response to God's amazing love is to love him in return, with all our heart, mind, soul and strength. God wants us to love him for who he is: not just for his love and mercy and goodness, but also as almighty God, creator of the universe, the lord of all, the one to whom all must give account. More importantly in his eyes, he wants us to love him as our own God, submitting to his authority in every matter, and joyfully taking our place among the people he looks after.

This requires both a once-and-for-all choice, and also daily choices. The decisive choice is to offer ourselves – the whole of us, every part – to God's service. We reject the option of letting any part of us serve evil purposes; ultimately that will lead to death, whereas the service of God results in life and light, holiness and happiness. If we are serving God, no-one else and nothing else can demand our services without God's agreement. But having made that decisive choice, we also need to make daily choices. Paul rejoices that the Christians in Rome have made the decisive choice and become obedient to God from the heart. Now they need to put that decision into practice, in the decisions of everyday life. Some of those decisions lead to dramatic changes in the direction of our lives. Others are just the myriad little things of life.

Frances (my wife) and I have had our share of these decisions. Probably the biggest one was the decision to offer ourselves for mission abroad. We had been challenged by a magazine article from a missionary society which had an opportunity to share the good news of Jesus to communities in West Africa. Whole villages were trying to decide whether to turn to Islam (the majority religion in the north of their country) or to Christianity (the majority religion in the south). They lived in between, and the idea was to send families to live among them so that they would see as well as hear the difference Jesus makes. But, that article lamented, no-one was willing to go. Why not? Well, that challenged us very strongly. Humanly speaking, we had every reason to stay. We had a very young family and our children had an elderly widowed grandfather living alone; and I was a fairly new vicar just beginning to see my ministry bearing fruit with some people deciding to follow Jesus. Surely God did not want us to go! But we felt uncomfortable with that assumption, and decided to check it out. We went to see the Society involved, and they pulled no punches – it wasn't safe, the children's education would be an issue, etc. etc.;

but the reward of seeing many people turning to Christ would be amazing. And it was an open door!

We both had made the decision to give ourselves wholly to Jesus (before we knew each other), and knew that if God wanted us to go, we had to go, whatever the risks. God would look after us and our families; and even if not, we still had to obey. Or should we be 'sensible' and say no? That was the battle in our hearts; in the end we said 'Yes' – and then God took us in a different direction, to serve with another missionary society (CMS). We ended up in Uganda for 5 years or so, a time with lovely experiences and also some horrendous ones; but God did indeed take care of us and the family.

We all also, of course, have the daily decisions of everyday life. Sometimes these are harder to get right – after all, do they really matter? They are such minor choices! Yet I am aware that what I need to offer to God's service is not just my hands and time etc., but my attitudes and my thinking. All too often I am governed by selfishness or pride, and then use my brain to justify myself. Or it may be that I do myself down, and think of myself as a failure or whatever, and not as a child of God, called to his high service. These parts of my life also need to be fully under the authority of my loving heavenly Father.

A verse that our church home group took to heart a little while back was Colossians 3:17: 'And, whatever you say or do, do everything in the name of the Lord Jesus; and through him offer thanksgiving to God the father.' To do something in the name of someone is to act as their representative; and we are Jesus' representative in all our words and deeds. What a privilege!

The result of serving Jesus this way is ever-increasing holiness, says Paul, and the end is eternal life: not a deserved wage for our service, but a free gift from God. When we sin, what we deserve is separation from God, eternal death – that is the 'wages' of sin. But when we believed, God gave us instead the free gift of union with Jesus in his death and in his resurrection. Amazing grace!

ROMANS CHAPTER 7

[1]Surely, friends, you know (for I am speaking to people who know what Law means) that Law has power over a person only as long as they live. [2]For example, by law a married woman is bound to her husband while he is living; but, if her husband dies, she is set free from the law that bound her to him. [3]If, then, during her husband's lifetime, she unites herself to another man, she will be called an adulteress; but, if her husband dies, the law has no further hold on her, nor, if she unites herself to another man, is she an adulteress. [4]And so with you, my friends; as far as the Law was concerned, you underwent death in the crucified body of the Christ, so that you might be united to another, to him who was raised from the dead, in order that our lives might bear fruit for God. [5]When we were living merely earthly lives, our sinful passions, aroused by the Law, were active in every part of our bodies, with the result that our lives bore fruit for death. [6]But now we are set free from the Law, because we are dead to that which once kept us under restraint; and so we serve under new,

spiritual conditions, and not under old, written regulations.

Earlier on, Paul asked the question, 'Are we to sin because we are living under the reign of love and not under the law?' (Romans 6:15.) Now he faces up to that question in more detail. His whole teaching so far is that we are righteous in God's eyes not through obedience to God's commands, but through faith in Jesus who took our sins upon himself. When we believe in Jesus, we are no longer under the law of God, as revealed in Scripture, with all its regulations and punishments for disobedience.

How can this be? That was a big question for Paul's readers, who were either Jews brought up going to the synagogue and taught the law there, or were non-Jews who were interested in the Jewish faith and had investigated the Jewish teachings and Scriptures. Was Paul saying that sin didn't matter – that we are not under the judgement of the law but under the reign of love and therefore we can do what the Jewish law forbade, without any fear of the consequences? Again, Paul answers by emphasising our union with Christ and what that means – especially our union with him in his death

He begins with the truth that dead people do not have to obey any laws. Death ends all legal requirements. He mentions marriage as a case in point – marriages end with the death of a partner, and the one who is left is free to remarry – a freedom that would have been against the law if the spouse was still alive. In a similar way the death of Christ frees us who are united to him from all obligations under the Old Testament laws, in order that we might 'belong to another, to him who was raised from the dead.' (I note that freedom from rules is not freedom to do what I want, but freedom to do what Jesus wants – I now belong to him.) God's purpose in uniting us with Christ is that 'our lives might bear fruit for God' – the fruit of right living, the 'ever-increasing holiness' that Paul mentioned earlier. The Law could not produce that fruit, because it taught us what wrong-doing was without enabling us to do right, and our human nature used this knowledge to explore sin rather than avoid it! The result was that we earned the wages of sin, death. Now, however, because of our union with Christ, we are dead as far as the Law of God is concerned, no longer forced to obey by the threat of punishment, but instead free to live lives that are fully pleasing to God. Paul will say more about this in chapter 8.

[7]What are we to say, then? That Law and sin are the same thing? Heaven forbid! On the contrary, I should not have learned what sin is, had not it been for Law. If the Law did not say "You must not covet," I should not know what it is to covet. [8]But sin took advantage of the commandment to arouse in me every form of covetousness, for where there is no consciousness of Law sin shows no sign of life. [9]There was a time when I myself, unconscious of Law, was alive; but when the commandment was brought home to me, sin sprang into life, while I died! [10]The commandment that should have meant life I found to result in death! [11]Sin took advantage of the commandment to deceive me, and used it to bring about my death. [12]And so the Law is holy,

and each commandment is also holy, and just, and good.

[13]Did, then, a thing, which in itself was good, involve death in my case? Heaven forbid! It was sin that involved death; so that, by its use of what I regarded as good to bring about my death, its true nature might appear; and in this way the commandment showed how intensely sinful sin is.

IF WE NEED TO BE SET free from the law of God in order to live with God and for God, does that mean that the law is now an evil to be got rid of? Paul is appalled at the suggestion. After all, the law that God gave to Moses was a revelation of the right way to live, and it also revealed a lot about God's nature and character – his holiness and his goodness and love for his people. The revelation of the right way to live at the same time revealed the wrong way to live – it brought to light what was sinful in the eyes of God. Paul illustrates this with the law against coveting – without it, 'I should not have known what it is to covet.' In other words, the law told Paul that coveting was wrong. That does not mean he never coveted anything before he heard of that law – even small children want things other children have. But he didn't 'know' it in the deepest sense: not just what it meant, and that it was forbidden, but how sinful it was. That knowledge did not stop him coveting; what it did was make him feel guilty – quite rightly – and that separated him from God. He died. The problem was not in the law, which is holy and just and good, but in himself, in his ordinary human nature which has a fatal attraction to wrong-doing. The human nature we're born with is unable to live a perfect life – 'We're only human,' is a common saying. Sin – missing the mark – is part and parcel of each one of us all our earthly lives. We're only saved from it completely when we receive our resurrection bodies. In the meantime, do I excuse sin by reflecting on how common it is and how relatively mild my sin is compared to others, or do I see 'how intensely sinful sin is', and hate it accordingly? Does my awareness of how God sees me as righteous soften my hatred of the sin that resides in my oh-so-human body?

[14]We know that the Law is spiritual, but I am earthly – sold into slavery to sin. [15]I do not understand my own actions. For I am so far from habitually doing what I want to do, that I find myself doing the thing that I hate. [16]But when I do what I want not to do, I am admitting that the Law is right. [17]This being so, the action is no longer my own, but is done by the sin which is within me. [18]I know that there is nothing good in me – I mean in my earthly nature. For, although it is easy for me to want to do right, to act rightly is not easy. [19]I fail to do the good thing that I want to do, but the bad thing that I want not to do – that I habitually do. [20]But, when I do the thing that I want not to do, the action is no longer my own, but is done by the sin which is within me. [21]This, then, is the law that I find – when I want to do right, wrong presents itself! [22]At heart I delight in the Law of God; [23]but throughout my body I see a different law, one which is in conflict with the law accepted by my reason, and which endeavours to make

me a prisoner to that law of sin which exists throughout my body. [24]Miserable man that I am! Who will deliver me from the body that is bringing me to this death? [25]Thank God, there is deliverance through Jesus Christ, our Lord! Well then, for myself, with my reason I serve the Law of God, but with my earthly nature the Law of sin.

THERE'S BEEN QUITE a debate in the past about whether Paul is referring to his experience before or after his conversion on the road to Damascus. He uses expressions which could be taken either way. He is 'sold into slavery to sin', 'there is nothing good in me', 'the body is bringing me to death' – all that sounds like a person without Jesus. But 'the action is no longer my own, but is done by the sin which is within me', 'At heart I delight in the Law of God', those statements sound like a converted person. I believe that he is talking in the present tense about his present experience – an experience I guess most Christians can identify with. St John in his first letter says that if anyone thinks they are without sin, they are deceiving themselves. And Paul himself, in his letter to the Galatians, talks about the way that our natural human nature (literally, our 'flesh') and the Holy Spirit within us are in conflict with each other, so that we do not do what we want to do. His advice to the Galatians is to keep in step with the Spirit, so that we do not follow the desires of our earthly nature. In this letter he will say something very similar in chapter 8; but in this passage he describes the conflict without mentioning the Holy Spirit – the conflict is between our earthly nature and our hearts.

The point is that when we believed in Jesus we were united to him spiritually, and partake of his new, resurrection, life – a life that is perfectly in tune with God. But this life is in our hearts and in our spirits, it hasn't yet transformed the physical bodies we were born with. I believe that all of us who die before Jesus returns will at that point say goodbye to our physical bodies; and our spirits, which have already been transformed, will go to be with Christ in paradise. If we have stayed alive until Jesus returns, we will see that all those who died in faith will at that point be resurrected with new bodies just like Jesus', and come to earth with him; we ourselves will not die and be resurrected, but our bodies will be transformed – this is Paul's teaching in 1 Thessalonians 4:11-18 and 1 Corinthians 15:51-54. Until then, we're stuck with the bodies we were born with, with all their frailties and sinful tendencies as well as their amazing reflections of God's image.

Paul describes his own experience, and his frustration at not being able to live the perfect life he longs for. What that life looks like is described by the written Law. (I think Paul is thinking about all God's commands found in the Scriptures.) His longing to be perfectly obedient is a tacit admission that the Law is right and good. But that longing comes from his heart – 'In my heart I delight in the Law of God' (v.22) – the centre of his being, his true inner self. And that proves to him that the fault is not with his new nature, but with his old sinful nature, his 'earthly nature'. That is still very much present, and shows itself in any short-comings, mistakes, wrong thoughts, words and deeds. That sinful earthly nature actively seeks to exert itself and dominate – temptations and old habits can be very strong. How can he be free? 'Who will deliver me?' There is an answer: Jesus Christ our Lord.

I would have thought that he should have immediately gone on to expand on that answer, which he does in chapter 8; but instead he summarises the conflict he's been talking about: 'With my reason I serve the Law of God, but with my earthly nature I serve the Law of sin.'

Paul is not against his physical body! It is where sin exerts its influence but, in itself, it is not to be despised – after all, God created it. So elsewhere he encourages Christians to look after themselves, and to treat their bodies with respect as residences of the Holy Spirit. He has already taught us to offer every part of our bodies to God as instruments of righteousness. But I know in my own experience that making such an offering doesn't get rid of temptation! This teaching in Romans 7 encourages me to believe that I am not alone in my struggle to live a joyful obedient life with Christ.

ROMANS CHAPTER 8

[1]There is, therefore, now no condemnation for those who are in union with Christ Jesus; [2]for through your union with Christ Jesus, the Law of the life-giving Spirit has set you free from the Law of sin and death. [3]What Law could not do, in so far as our earthly nature weakened its action, God did, by sending his own Son, with a nature resembling our sinful nature, to atone for sin. He condemned sin in that earthly nature, [4]so that the requirements of the Law might be satisfied in us who live now in obedience, not to our earthly nature, but to the Spirit.

'There is, therefore, now no condemnation for those who are in union with Christ Jesus.' Why does Paul say 'therefore'? How is this statement a consequence of what he has just written in chapter 7? To answer that, we need to look back to the beginning of chapter 7, when he reminded us that in union with Christ Jesus we have died to the law, and now the law has no power over us to control us or condemn us – 'we serve under new, spiritual conditions, and not under old, written regulations' (Romans 7:6). The law teaches us how terrible sin is, and shows up the sinfulness that infects our earthly nature (literally our 'flesh'); but it does not affect our relationship with God – that is dependent on our union with Jesus, who lives in us through his Holy Spirit. The prophets had predicted, centuries before, that God would take away our heart of stone and give us a heart of flesh, and that there would be a new covenant, a new relationship with God, in which God's way of life would be natural to us (his law would be 'written on our hearts') – see Ezekiel 36:25-27 and Jeremiah 31:31-33. This is 'the Law of the life-giving Spirit', which sets us free from the law of sin and death. We who believe in Jesus are new covenant people.

Paul sums up what he has been saying earlier in the letter – that God sent Jesus to become a human like us in order to take responsibility for our sin and take upon himself the punishment we deserve. Since Jesus has already paid the penalty in full, there is now no condemnation for us who are united with him through our faith in him. No condemnation from God, and therefore no guilt; and therefore any condemnation we receive from other people – or ourselves – is not admissible in God's court of justice, which is the only court that really matters!

During my time as a student at university I read that some preachers whom God used to bring revival spent hours reading the Bible – George Whitefield would start at 5am! So I decided to do the same, getting up at 5 and reading my way through the Bible – or trying to. It was such a struggle to keep awake! Eventually it became too much of a burden for me to bear, and wasn't bringing me any closer to God. I needed to stop. However, I felt that if I stopped I would be condemned by God and myself as a failure. So I talked to a mature Christian from another university about it. I knew Romans 8:1, and knew in theory that there was no condemnation for those who are united to Christ; but I felt I needed to hear someone tell me that, in no uncertain terms. So

I angled the conversation to try to get him to say those words! Eventually he did so – and I felt such a release! The burden had been lifted.

Paul's point is more than that God will never condemn us when we live in union with Christ. He adds further perspectives: Jesus' death 'condemned sin in our earthly nature', giving our 'earthly nature' the sentence it deserved – death – so that even though we still live with that nature we are not enslaved to its every desire, but can live lives that are fully pleasing to God. As Romans 7 makes plain, our freedom from our old nature's power does not mean we no longer feel its sinful desires, and we can still make wrong choices (though God does not condemn us for doing so); but we now live with the Spirit and are able to obey him and do what God wants. We are united to Jesus! The whole purpose of removing our guilt is so that we can live! Live in his presence, live with the Holy Spirit in us, guiding and empowering us, live lives that are fully pleasing to him.

⁵They who follow their earthly nature are earthly-minded, while they who follow the Spirit are spiritually minded. ⁶To be earthly-minded means death, to be spiritually minded means life and peace; ⁷because to be earthly-minded is to be an enemy to God, for such a mind does not submit to the Law of God, nor indeed can it do so. ⁸They who are earthly cannot please God.

THE OLDER TRANSLATIONS of this passage use the words 'flesh' or 'carnal', where this translation uses the word 'earthly'. I like the word 'earthly', for Paul is talking about more than bodily appetite. I am 'earthly-minded' when my focus is on my own needs and desires without reference to God. My desires may often coincide with God's; God wants me to have food and clothing and the necessities of life, and he wants me to be concerned about the poor, and about issues like climate change and good government. But when I ignore God's desires and seek first my own fulfilment rather than the kingdom of God, I am being earthly-minded.

To be earthly-minded is not a light matter. Since it is ignoring God's will, it is denying God's authority, denying God's very nature as God. To be earthly-minded is to be against God, that is, to be an enemy of God; and the end result of such enmity is to be cut off from God who is the source of life.

The alternative to being earthly-minded is to be spiritually minded, following the guidance of the Holy Spirit, living in obedience to him. When our focus is on pleasing God in this way, we are satisfying the requirements of the Law (v. 4), and the result is life and peace, even if in our desire to please God we often fall short. There is no condemnation for those who live in this way.

[9]You, however, are not earthly but spiritual, since the Spirit of God lives within you. Unless a person has the Spirit of Christ, they do not belong to Christ; [10]but, if Christ is within you, then, though the body is dead as a consequence of sin, the spirit is life as a consequence of righteousness. [11]And, if the Spirit of him who raised Jesus from the dead lives within you, he who raised

Christ Jesus from the dead will give life even to your mortal bodies, through his Spirit living within you.

PAUL IS CONVINCED THAT the Romans he is writing to are indeed Christians, and that the Holy Spirit is living in them and they are following him – they are not earthly but spiritual. The importance of knowing and obeying the Holy Spirit cannot be underestimated. 'Unless a person has the Spirit of Christ, they do not belong to Christ.' I find it significant how in these verses the Holy Spirit is described both as 'the Spirit of God' and 'the Spirit of Christ', and that when the Spirit of Christ is living within us, Christ is within us – Paul already reflects the theology of the Triune, Three-in-One God that is such a central part of Christianity, even though he never uses the word 'Trinity'. It is also interesting to me that Paul sees the presence of the Holy Spirit as the proof that a person belongs to Christ; he expects Christians to know from experience that the Holy Spirit is in them. (We see this also in Galatians 3:2-5.)

When I first committed my life to Christ I was told that my faith in Jesus was the proof that I belonged to Christ, and that if I belonged to Christ I must have the Holy Spirit in me, even though I didn't recognise his presence in my experience. The presence of the Holy Spirit seemed to me to be theoretical rather than experiential. When, a few years later, I went to a Pentecostal church and started 'speaking in tongues' (one of the gifts of the Spirit in 1 Corinthians 12), probably my main source of joy was the knowledge that the Holy Spirit was real, and was in me. I wonder whether many Christians' belief that they lack the experience of the Holy Spirit is due to a lack of teaching about what that experience is like. For example, we learn in the next few verses that one of the things the Holy Spirit does is to give us the sense that God is our loving Father; many have that sense but don't know it is from the Holy Spirit. The gifts of the Spirit do indeed reveal the presence of the Holy Spirit; but 1 Corinthians 12 makes plain that gifts differ – not everyone speaks in tongues – and again, I wonder whether many Christians' sense that they lack any gifts of the Spirit is due to a lack of teaching.

Is it possible for us to be 'earthly minded' if the Holy Spirit is living in us? Paul has just told the Roman believers that the presence of the Spirit in them meant that they were spiritual, not earthly. I'm sure it is possible for spiritual people to slip at times into an earthly mindset; but the Holy Spirit will not abandon them but will keep nudging them back to Jesus. We are growing more like Jesus. Our bodies may be 'dead as a consequence of sin' – mortal, unfit for the world to come, unable to live in the presence of our holy God – but our spirits have been made new and eternal, because God has recreated them with the same sort of life that Jesus was raised to life with. Our spirits are united with Christ in his righteousness, and are fit for the new age, fit for the presence of God as shown by the fact that Christ now lives with our spirits in the person of the Holy Spirit. And this has an effect on our bodily life. The spirit of a person drives their actions; and our spirits work with the Holy Spirit to control the natural instincts of our mortal bodies, so that in this mortal life we live with and for God.

¹²So then, friends, we owe nothing to our earthly nature, that we should live in obedience to it. ¹³If you live in obedience to your earthly nature, you will

inevitably die; but if, by the power of the Spirit, you put an end to the evil habits of the body, you will live.

[14]All who are guided by the Spirit of God are children of God. [15]For you did not receive the spirit of a slave, to fill you once more with fear, but the spirit of a child by adoption, which leads us to cry "Abba, our Father."

CHRISTIANS HAVE FREE choice. We can choose to go along with our earthly desires or to follow the leading of the Holy Spirit within us. Both our earthly desires and the Holy Spirit are not merely giving advice or guidance; they are issuing commands, and our choice is which one to obey. Their commands come with promises: our earthly nature promises satisfaction and self-fulfilment; the Holy Spirit promises life in all its fullness. Paul points out that the promises of our earthly nature are lies: any satisfaction or sense of fulfilment from following its desires are only temporary; the end is death in all its fullness. Following the Holy Spirit involves putting 'an end to the evil habits of the body'. (Other versions say something like 'if you live according to the flesh you will die, but if by the Spirit you put to death the deeds of the body you will live.') We put an end to the evil habits of the body by the power of the Spirit, not by our own power and efforts; and the way this is done is explained in Galatians 5, where Paul says, 'Let your steps be guided by the Spirit, and then you will never gratify the cravings of your earthly nature'. We put our old cravings to death by neglect – ignoring them and focusing instead on the desires of the Spirit. That is the way of life of God's children. And as we seek to put that into practice, we find that the Holy Spirit deals with the desires and temptations of our earthly nature – sometimes dramatically, as when some addicts find immediate relief from their addiction, but more usually it seems to be a gradual process. We will never be free from temptation in this mortal life, but we will always have the power to ignore it. (Our earthly nature is not the only source of temptation; the devil and his minions will always be at work, but can be commanded in the name of Jesus to go – or simply laughed out of court, the devil hates that; and the world around us is also a source of temptation to be resisted – in union with Christ the world has been crucified to us, and us to the world, Galatians 6:14.)

All who are guided by the Holy Spirit are children of God. That's easy to say; but what a huge statement it is! God has adopted us, and that means we have all the privileges and status of full family members. In Roman society, a man could adopt even a slave, and make that adopted person the inheritor of his whole estate. Julius Caesar adopted Octavian as his son and heir, who eventually became the emperor Augustus. An adopted child was in no way inferior to a natural child. So to say we are adopted children of God is truly stupendous! It may be possible for an adopted child to be loved less than a natural child, but if we are united with the Son of God through faith and his Spirit lives in us, God loves us with the love he has for Jesus. We are deeply loved children of God! We know that God loves every person in a deep and personal way, even if they don't believe in him and live as his enemies, and will end up reaping the reward of sin. But he loves us who follow Jesus and are guided by the Holy Spirit in a special way, because we are now family members and he is our Father.

Paul's mention that we did not receive the spirit of a slave, to fill us once more with fear, is important – and a great relief. I find that at times I am obeying God out of a sense of duty, fearing lest I displease him, even though I know that there is no condemnation for me – deep down I really do love God. Jesus said, "If you love me, you will lay my commands to heart" (John 14:15), but I often interpret that as 'if I keep Jesus' commands, that counts as love for him', which can drive a slavish kind of obedience and an anxiety about falling short. That does not come from the Holy Spirit, but from my earthly nature. The Holy Spirit is the Spirit of loving trust in our loving heavenly Father – 'Abba' was the way a child addressed their fathers, an equivalent of the English 'Daddy' (but possibly with a little more respect than we might have had!). We do not obey out of fear of punishment – as 1 John 4:18 says, 'There is no fear in love; perfect love drives out fear because fear has to do with punishment. So anyone who is afraid has not reached perfection in love.' We love and obey, because God first loved us and has given us new hearts and his holy Spirit. It is the Holy Spirit of God who gives us that sense that we are beloved children of God, and kindles in us loving obedience – the natural response to his loving guidance.

A deep sense of God as our loving heavenly Father may not come as soon as we believe in Jesus, as I know from my own experience. One evening when we were on leave during our time as missionaries in Uganda I went on my own to visit a supporting church to update them on how we were getting on. I was invited to a home group, and that group asked if they could pray for me. I can't remember all the details, but the upshot was that they decided to pray for my relationship with my father, whom I loved and admired, but who had worked in Nigeria until I was 13. That meant there were times when he was there and we children were at boarding school here in the UK. I didn't feel there was any problem with our relationship, but I let them pray for me and afterwards returned home, thinking nothing of it. However, a few days later

I was alone having a time of prayer in the house while everyone else was out shopping. Suddenly, out of the blue, I sensed 'loud and clear' that God was saying to me, "You are my beloved son." That experience awakened in me a new sense of God the Father as my own loving, heavenly Father. I think I already had a good relationship with the Holy Spirit and with Jesus, but was not so close to God the Father; this experience redressed the balance, perhaps!

[16]The Spirit himself unites with our spirits in bearing witness to our being God's children, [17]and if children, then heirs – heirs of God, and joint heirs with Christ, since we share Christ's sufferings in order that we may also share his glory.

PAUL NOW GOES ON TO affirm that we are not only children of God, but also heirs of God, joint heirs with Christ. What does that mean? Nowadays we regard an heir as someone who inherits the property of their parent after that parent's death. In the Bible it has a broader meaning.

In the Old Testament the inheritance was the land promised by God to the Jewish ancestors, and distributed by lot to the different tribes, so each tribe had a certain proportion of the promised land as their inheritance. Each family had a share, a parcel of land taken from their tribal lands, and that parcel was the inheritance of every generation of that family – all the children were heirs of their family inheritance. (Girls, when they married, left their family inheritance to become part of their husband's family.) Sometimes the Bible says that Israel is God's inheritance – not that he took possession of it when his father died (God has never had a Father!), but that the land, and especially the people of Israel, are his possession, are where his home is. But there was always a sense that the promises were yet to be fulfilled in all their glory; the land was seldom a place of peace, and the Israelites seldom lived up to their calling to be God's special people.

In the New Testament that idea of inheritance is broadened further, and usually refers to the Kingdom of God ('the Kingdom of Heaven' in Matthew's gospel). Jesus, the Son of God, inherits the Kingdom of God; that does not mean that God the Father has to die, but that the Kingdom becomes his property, he becomes the King. That has already happened: Jesus told his disciples before he left earth to ascend to heaven, 'All authority in heaven and on the earth has been given to me' (Matthew 28:18). He is now in the process of transforming heaven and earth to bring in the Kingdom of God in all its fullness, and it is that future Kingdom that is the true 'promised land'. The transformation will include the removal of all evil; but that, I believe, first needs evil to be revealed in its true colours. That is the stage we are now living in: modern communications reveal more and more evil alongside the growth of faith in King Jesus across the world (even if we don't see so much growth in our own country).

We are now the children of God, and that means we share in the inheritance of the Kingdom of God. We are joint heirs with Christ, since he is now the King of God's Kingdom and we are united to him and have his Spirit within us. We too are now the inheritors of the 'promised land', the new creation that God is going to establish. We have an inheritance that is 'imperishable, stainless, unfading,' 'reserved for you in heaven', 'ready to be revealed in the last days' (1 Peter 1:3-5). This inheritance will be God's home, Jesus' home, and our home too – we will live for ever in the presence of God, where there is no suffering or unhappiness, only glory and joy. But (and it is quite a big 'but',) the joy that is to come is preceded by suffering, just as Christ suffered when he left all the glory of heaven to become a baby at Bethlehem, a refugee in Egypt, a bread-winner in the Nazareth carpenter's shop, a homeless preacher during his years of ministry during which he experienced not only the adulation of the crowds, but also their hostility and that of the authorities, leading to his trial, crucifixion and death. Our trials are not identical, but we share with Jesus the suffering of living in a sinful world; and Paul tells us that this suffering is a necessary part of the journey to the Promised Land. As he said in chapter 5, suffering produces character and hope – and that hope does not disappoint us, because the love of God has been poured out into our hearts through the Holy Spirit.

18I do not count the sufferings of our present life worthy of mention when compared with the glory that is to be revealed and bestowed on us. 19All nature awaits with eager expectation the appearing of the sons of God. 20For nature was made subject to imperfection – not by its own choice, but owing to him who made it so – 21yet not without the hope that some day nature, also, will be set free from enslavement to decay, and will attain to the freedom which will mark the glory of the children of God. 22We know, indeed, that all nature alike has

been groaning in the pains of labour to this very hour.

²³And not nature only; but we ourselves also, though we have already a first gift of the Spirit – we ourselves are inwardly groaning, while we eagerly await our full adoption as sons – the redemption of our bodies. ²⁴By our hope we were saved. But the thing hoped for is no longer an object of hope when it is before our eyes; for who hopes for what is before his eyes? ²⁵But when we hope for what is not before our eyes, then we wait for it with patience.

WHAT IS THE FUTURE for our world? Paul's answer: unimaginable bliss! We may be suffering now – some of us unbearably. Paul had experienced much suffering himself; he had at times despaired of life (2 Corinthians 1:8). However, he is convinced that our future joy will immeasurably make up for any suffering we experience: 'The light burden of our momentary trouble is preparing for us a weight of imperishable glory, beyond all measure' (2 Corinthians 4:17). He is looking forward to great glory, a glory commensurate with our status as children of God, God's royal family. In this world our status and glory is hidden, as is Christ's; but when Jesus is revealed at his return to earth – revealed in great glory with a retinue of angels (Matthew 25:31) – we too will be revealed as the amazing people we really are by God's grace (Colossians 3:3,4). I would love to know what exactly that glory will look like. The Bible tells us that we will have important roles in the new creation (e.g. 1 Corinthians 5:3) – and presumably we will have the abilities to match, so that whatever responsibilities we have will be a joy, not a burden – and that would be at least part of what Paul means when he says we have been seated with Christ on high (Ephesians 2:3). However, he does not elaborate here on the glory to come, except to say how it will affect all nature.

I love the way Paul gives nature a personality – waiting with eager longing! Hardly scientific language, but Paul was no scientist! He sees the cycle of life and death as a problem; the word translated 'imperfection' means futility, emptiness, purposelessness. Nature itself is subject to futility by God's will. Paul may have been thinking back to the story of the Garden of Eden and God's curse on the ground because of Adam's sin, assuming that the curse was not just on the vegetation but on the whole of nature. But he does not say so, and he does not make the obvious connection with Adam, so I take it at face value, that God intended nature to be trapped in the cycle of decay and life – in this world, the cycle of life depends on including death and decay. Yet that is not the end of the story – there is a better world to come, when nature will be set free from decay and itself experience the 'freedom which will mark the glory of the children of God'. What that freedom consists of Paul does not spell out; for us it includes freedom from sin and freedom from death and decay, pain and suffering, and freedom to be the people God intends us to be, living life in all its fullness. I guess nature will experience a lot of that, and will itself experience life in all its fullness, according to its myriad forms, and the biological system will not need death and decay. I am looking forward to seeing what that will look like!

Paul uses the image of childbirth – a painful process (naturally) with a happy purpose, the beginning of a new life on earth. Nature is going through the pains of childbirth, and the result will be new creation. That to me implies some kind of continuity: God is not making a new creation out of nothing, after the old creation is ended. The old creation is producing the new. So it is with us humans: we too are experiencing pain and suffering, but that too is the pain of childbirth, and the intended result is new creation. Our bodies will be redeemed, set free from their mortality; they will still be bodies with flesh and bones, as Jesus had after his resurrection, and I do believe that in some way they will reflect what we have become in this present life, just as Jesus' resurrection body retained the marks of his loving sacrifice for us. Our present affects our future. In a similar way, I believe the future affects – or should affect – our present. Peter says in 2 Peter 3:11,12, 'What holy and pious lives you ought to lead, while you wait for the coming of the day of God and strive to make it come soon.'

One aspect of this must be our relationship to the present creation. Psalm 8 points to God's intention that all things, including all animals, birds and fish, should be under human authority; Hebrews 2 comments that we don't see that at the moment, but we do see it fulfilled in Jesus. Since we are united to Jesus and will reign with him in the new creation (2 Timothy 2:12), we too will have responsibility for caring for it; and since we have that new creation life in our spirits, that should radically affect the way we live our present life in relationship with the rest of creation. It also affects the way we live with each other – so much of the New Testament is taken up with explaining how in this world we are to live the new life we've been given.

The Holy Spirit's presence in us is the guarantee that the redemption of our bodies will take place; but we have to be patient. Paul calls what we are waiting for our 'adoption as sons'. (I'm sure that nowadays he would use more inclusive language, though writing to the Romans the idea of adopting daughters wouldn't have occurred to him since that probably didn't happen in those days.) But it is interesting to me that our adoption has already happened, and the Spirit witnesses to our spirits that we are God's children; and yet our adoption is yet to happen! We are already fully children of God, but do not yet experience that in all its fullness – we need to be new creations not only in spirit but in every aspect of our being – body, mind, feelings, spirit.

'By our hope we are saved'. Our faith is not only faith in Jesus' love and in his death and resurrection; it is also faith in his promised future for us and for nature. 'If all that we have done has been to place our hope in Christ for this life, then we of all people are the most to be pitied' (1 Corinthians 15:19). This future has not yet arrived – if it had, it would not be hope but knowledge. Our hope is strong and certain – not wishful thinking – because it is based on Jesus' life and character. The experience of the Holy Spirit is not scientific proof of what is to come, although his presence is such a reassurance and help. We live by faith, not by sight.

²⁶So, also, the Spirit supports us in our weakness. We do not even know how to pray as we should; but the Spirit himself pleads for us in sighs that can find no utterance.

²⁷Yet he who searches all our hearts knows what the Spirit's meaning is, because the pleadings of the Spirit for Christ's people are in accordance with his will.

ONE OF THE WAYS THE Holy Spirit helps us is by praying for us. This is amazing! And also a bit of a puzzle – how is it that the Spirit of God needs to pray to God for things that God already knows we need? Does our loving God need his arm twisted? Surely not! I suspect the answer to this lies in the inner workings of the Trinity, which are of course hidden from us. I wonder if the Holy Spirit's work can in part be illustrated by the work of our nervous system: just as the nerves transmit signals to the brain, and the brain sends signals to our muscles through the nerves, so the Holy Spirit, present everywhere in the world but present in a special way in us, is the agent of God the Father, the 'Go-between God' as someone once put it, a spiritual nervous system linking us to the Father, and his pleading for us is him transmitting 'signals' to our Father in heaven, communicating with him about us with deep empathy. Pure speculation, of course! It may also be something to do with the importance God puts on prayer, so that even Jesus the Son of God needed to keep in touch with the Father through prayer, and the Holy Spirit speaks directly to the Father about things we ourselves need but don't ask for, or ask for mistakenly.

Whatever the answer is, it is plain that the Holy Spirit is pleading for us, and that his pleading is in accordance with the Father's will; and that, although we aren't aware of what's going on, the Father knows exactly what the Spirit is asking for, and we are being looked after in a far deeper sense than we know. We do not know how to pray as we should; but that is not a problem to God, and – through the Holy Spirit – he knows what we need before we ask it, even if we don't know what to ask for or how to ask it.

28But we do know that God causes all things to work together for the good of those who love him – those who have received the call in accordance with his

purpose. [29]For those whom God chose from the first he also destined from the first to be transformed into likeness to his Son, so that his Son might be the eldest among many brothers and sisters. [30]And those whom God destined for this he also called; and those whom he called he also pronounced righteous; and those whom he pronounced righteous he also brought to glory.

GOD CARES FOR US. We don't really know how to pray (the 'we' includes Saint Paul himself!), but we do know that God causes all things to work together for the good of those who love him. The 'all things' include all the bad things Paul is about to mention – trouble, persecution, poverty, danger, death. In all things God is working for our good if we are his people, for he is working all things together to accomplish his good purposes for his children and for all of nature. We are God's adopted children, and adopted children are chosen ones, chosen by their adoptive parents. In Roman society a landowner may adopt a slave and give him the inheritance above his natural child if he doesn't trust the latter to look after the estate; he adopts the slave for a purpose. And we too have been chosen for a purpose: Jesus said to his disciples, 'It wasn't you who chose me, but I who chose you, and I appointed you to go and bear fruit – fruit that should remain' (John 15:16). That fruit is above all Christ-likeness: God chose us 'to be transformed into likeness to his Son.' And that transformation was also for a purpose: that God the Father would have a huge family, all bearing the family likeness.

There has been a lot of argument over the ages about this teaching that God has 'chosen' us. If God is sovereign, who can resist his will? If God is sovereign, do we really have free will? I think the problem is that we cannot get our heads around those two seemingly contradictory facts. Yet the same problem is there in human life: human behaviour can be predictable, without us feeling that our behaviour is inevitable or that we are not accountable for our actions. In John 15 Jesus warns that those who do not produce fruit will be cut out of the Vine, and the thrust of his teaching there is that we should remain in him, and obey his commands – especially the command to love one another. Some theologians distinguish between a 'calling' and an 'effectual calling'. 'Many are called, but few are chosen' said Jesus (Matthew 22:14). Only if the calling results in a committed response can it be called 'effectual'. God's destiny for his children is eternal life as members of his family, and Paul tells us that God wants everyone on earth to reach that destiny (1 Timothy 2:4). But, much to God's grief, most people are on a 'road that leads to destruction' (Matthew 7:13). If we love God now, the teaching in these verses is very encouraging and reassuring. But we cannot take our destiny for granted, and assume we are safe and can now go our own way. We are indeed safe, if we remain united to Christ, and keep growing in Christ-likeness; and if we love God we can be sure he is working all things together for our good – even those things which are the result of our or other people's free choice!

I am writing this at a time when there is terrible conflict in Israel and Palestine, with many thousands of civilians dead or injured, including thousands of children. How can God be working for good in this situation? I don't know. But I do know that God causes all things to work together for the good of those who love him. Perhaps it will make better sense from an eternal perspective, given the fact that there is an age to come, that justice will be done and that God's kindness and grace will far outweigh the pain we experience here and now. We also know that little children have a special place in the heart of God. We also know that God is the giver of peace, and in the end peace will reign. But we don't sit back and resign ourselves to 'fate'. We join with the Holy Spirit in pleading with the Father.

[31]What are we to say, then, in the light of all this? If God is on our side, who can there be against us? [32]God did not withhold his own Son, but gave him up on behalf of us all; will he not, then, with him, freely give us all things? [33]Who will bring a charge against any of God's people? He who pronounces them righteous is God! [34]Who is there to condemn them? He who died for us is Christ Jesus! – or, rather, it was he who was raised from the dead, and who is now at God's right hand and is even pleading on our behalf! [35]Who is there to separate us from the love of the Christ? Will trouble, or difficulty, or persecution, or hunger, or nakedness, or danger, or the sword? [36]Scripture says – "For your sake we are being killed all the day long, we are regarded as sheep to be slaughtered." [37]Yet amid all these things we more than conquer through him who loved us! [38]For I am persuaded that neither death, nor life, nor angels, nor archangels, nor the present, nor the future, nor any powers, [39]nor height, nor depth, nor any other created

thing, will be able to separate us from the love of God revealed in Christ Jesus, our Lord.

GOD IS ON OUR SIDE! Literally, 'God is on behalf of us' – he is not just backing us, but acting on our behalf. He gave his own Son to act on our behalf, dying for us and rising to new life for us. Some people think God was doing something bad by sending his Son to a terrible death; yet this was the supreme sacrifice, the supreme expression of love for us sinful people, a love fully shared by his Son who was all too willing to become our representative and die for us – 'Though the divine nature was his from the beginning, yet he did not look on equality with God as above all things to be clung to, but impoverished himself by taking the nature of a servant and becoming like one of us; he appeared among us as a man, and still further humbled himself by submitting even to death – to death on a cross!' (Philippians 2:6-8). If this is how God loves us, then who can be against us? If God loves us so much that he gave us his only Son, then nothing else is too much for God to give us – to give us freely, without asking whether we deserve it or not! (Paul uses one word for 'freely give', a word derived from the one we translate 'grace'.) So when we do not receive answers to our prayers, it is not because God has stopped loving us, or is wanting to punish us. As Paul goes on, 'Who will bring a charge against any of God's people?... Who is there to condemn them?'

I need to hear this. So often the one who brings a charge against me, who condemns me, is I myself. I am only too aware of my own failings and shortcomings, for example in lack of attentiveness to people I am having a conversation with, and lack of attentiveness to God himself in worship situations. But if God pronounces me righteous, who am I to say I am not? If God says there is no charge

I or anyone can lay against me, that settles the matter: I am righteous, whatever others might think! Jesus does not condemn me, even when he bore my sins – because he bore my sins! Nor does he condemn me for my feelings of condemnation (that makes me laugh!) – he is at the right hand side of God, in the position of ultimate power and authority, and he is 'pleading on my behalf'. He understands! (Paul told us earlier in this chapter that the Holy Spirit pleads for Christ's people – I think this is an example of the unity within the Trinity!)

'Who is there to separate us from the love of the Christ?' When we are in trouble or difficulty, facing persecution, facing famine, poverty, danger, death, does that mean Jesus the Messiah has stopped loving us? No! Paul had experienced all these things, and knew more than ever that Jesus loved him. He does not mention sin in this list – he has already taught us that our sin has been forgiven through the love of Jesus. There is nothing in all creation, no experience we can ever have, that can separate us from the love of God that is in Christ Jesus for us. We 'overconquer' through Jesus and his love – not that we are rescued from all these things in this life, but that the one we trust, our Saviour who loves us, will see us through them to the final victory when he returns to put an end to all sin and suffering and reward us who have remained faithfully following him as best we can. We are united to Jesus, who has overcome sin and death on our behalf and, when he appears, we too will appear with him in glory (Colossians 3:4).

When we are walking in the darkness, and experiencing conflict or suffering or grief in any way, it is difficult, even impossible, to feel loved by God. Nevertheless, the truth remains: nothing can separate us, who are united to Jesus by faith, from

God's love. We live by faith, not by sight or feeling. God is for us! God loves us so much!

ROMANS CHAPTER 9

[1]I am speaking the truth as one in union with Christ; it is no lie; and my conscience, enlightened by the Holy Spirit, [2]bears me out when I say that there is a great weight of sorrow on me and that my heart is never free from pain. [3]I could wish that I were myself accursed and severed from the Christ, for the sake of my people – my own flesh and blood. [4]For they are Israelites, and theirs are the adoption as children, the visible presence, the covenants, the revealed Law, the Temple worship, and the promises. [5]They are descended from the patriarchs, and, as far as his human nature was concerned, from them came the Christ – he who is supreme over all things, God for ever blessed. Amen.

Paul uses amazingly strong language here, as if he expects his readers to doubt the truth of what he is about to say. He has just been saying that no trouble or persecution or danger can separate us from the love of God in Christ. What is he about to say that demands such an introduction as we have here?

I think the list of difficulties that he's just mentioned at the end of the last chapter reminds him that in his case they all stem from the opposition of his own people, the Jews. Wherever he travelled on his missionary journeys he met with violent antagonism, not from the non-Jewish population, but from his fellow Jews. His readers would expect him to react with some kind of invective against those Jews; so what he goes on to say would come as a complete surprise. He loved his own people! He wants them to believe in Jesus as their longed-for Messiah, the Christ! So much so that he wished he could himself be separated from the love of God if that would result in their salvation! He loves them so much that their rejection of Jesus fills him with 'a great weight of sorrow', and his 'heart is never free from pain'.

That expression of pain amazes me – how does it fit in with Paul's encouragement to exult in our hope, and even to exult in our troubles (chapter 5:1-3)? In his list of the fruit of the Spirit the second item after love is joy – how can we be joyful if, like Paul, we are never free from pain? In this letter he has given other expressions of pain – 'Miserable man that I am' (7:24); 'We are regarded as sheep to be slaughtered' (8:36). Yet in 1 Thessalonians 4:16 he says, 'Always be joyful.' How? Can we feel joy and pain at the same time?

I wonder if the answer lies in what Paul says in Colossians 2:1-4: 'Since, therefore, you were raised to life with the Christ, seek for the things that are above; for it is there that the Christ is seated at the right hand of God. Fix your thoughts on the things that are above, not on those that are on earth. For you died, and your life now lies hidden, with the Christ, in God. When the Christ, who is our life, appears, then you also will appear with him in glory.' Jesus the Messiah is with God in glory, and we are united to him even now; in the future we will enjoy with him all the glories of the new creation. What we are to do now is to 'fix our thoughts on the things that are above'. That can't mean that we stop thinking about anything here on earth; that would be impossible. What it must mean is that we need in a sense to anchor our lives in Christ, or to change the metaphor, to be like deep sea divers whose life-lines go up to the boat on the surface. Those divers concentrate on the tasks they are doing, and react to what's in front of them, yet all the time are aware of their connection to the surface and the air above. Our connection with Christ is an amazingly joyful one. His is the spiritual air we breathe! But we react to the things in front of us, and that is usually a mixture of good and evil – the evil can fill us with sorrow, and the good with joy. So I can be very sad at the experiences I or the people I'm with or am thinking about are having, while at the same time being aware of my joyful connection to Jesus, and can be happy about the good things I see. I can count my blessings while at the same time feeling pain and sorrow – those troubles cannot overwhelm me if I am united to Christ, as Paul has just written in Romans 8. So Paul is filled with sorrow at his people's rejection of Jesus; but it is not because of the persecution he suffers from them, but because they are missing God's good purposes for them.

Why does he want his people's salvation so much? I believe it was because he knew that God loved them so much – they were, and still are, his chosen people. They were incredibly privileged. God had promised their ancestor Abraham that through his descendants the whole world would be blessed. God had entered into covenant with them that he would be their God and they would be his people. God called the nation Israel his 'son' (Hosea 11:1) – 'theirs are the adoption as children', says Paul – they too have the right to call God 'Father', and had that right long before us who are not Jews. God had revealed to them his ways, he had given them access to him through the temple worship (this letter was written decades before the temple was destroyed), and God had given them amazing promises about his plans for their future. Above all, Jesus the Messiah, who has all authority in heaven and earth, was himself a Jew.

The Jews no longer have the temple. The Romans razed it to the ground, and where the temple was is today within the compound of the Al-Aqsa mosque. But the Jews are still God's chosen people. And that remains true despite the horrific slaughter by Israel of thousands of civilians and innocent children in Gaza at the time of writing, as they respond to the even more horrific slaughter of Israeli civilians by Hamas. We who are Christians cannot pretend to be 'holier than thou'. We may not agree with the ways Jews have behaved in the past, we may not approve of the way Palestinians are being treated in the Middle East today – but have we behaved any better? How can anyone justify the horrors of the ways so-called Christians have treated the Jews in the last two thousand years? It is possible to be against the actions of the Israeli government without being anti-Semitic, just as Paul hated the suffering caused by the persecution he was enduring yet loved his enemies and wanted their salvation. No Christian should be anti-Semitic (nor anti any other people group). The Jews were and are still God's people, and Paul now goes on to talk about God's plan for them.

⁶Not that God's Word has failed. For it is not all who are descended from Israel who are true Israelites; ⁷nor, because they are Abraham's descendants, are they all his children; but – "It is Isaac's children who will be called your descendants." ⁸This means that it is not the

children born in the course of nature who are God's children, but it is the children born in fulfilment of the promise who are to be regarded as Abraham's descendants. ^{9}For these words are the words of a promise – "About this time I will come, and Sarah will have a son." ^{10}Nor is that all. There is also the case of Rebecca, when she was about to bear children to our ancestor Isaac. ^{11}For in order that the purpose of God, working through selection, might not fail – a selection depending, not on obedience, but on his call – Rebecca was told, before her children were born and before they had done anything either right or wrong, ^{12}that the elder would be a servant to the younger. ^{13}The words of scripture are – "I loved Jacob, but I hated Esau."

THE FACT THAT THE JEWS are God's chosen people does not absolve them from responsibility for all their wrong-doing. They need to be saved from their sin. Paul passionately wants his fellow Jews to receive salvation through faith in Jesus. However, he knows that the vast majority reject the idea that Jesus is their Messiah. As he thinks of the promise God made to Abraham that he would be God to him and to his descendants after him, he realises that not every descendant would be included. Abraham's son Isaac would be included, but not his son Ishmael, whose mother was not Sarah but Sarah's slave girl. Isaac's son Jacob would be included but not Esau – and that decision was made before they were born. God chose who would be counted as his people, and who would not, before any of them deserved anything. In this letter Paul is at pains to emphasise that all who believe in Jesus are included as God's people, not on the basis of anything we have done, but by God's own choice – his love for us is wholly undeserved. It's grace.

When Paul quotes the Scripture, 'I loved Jacob but I hated Esau', he is merely emphasising God's activity in choosing – Jacob was chosen, Esau was not. (Paul was quoting from the prophet Malachi, who lived after the Babylonians had destroyed Jerusalem and exiled the descendants of Jacob. The Babylonians were in turn conquered by the Persians, who allowed the Jews to return and rebuild Jerusalem. Malachi saw that the people of Edom, descendants of Esau, had not fared so well.) Esau seems to many people the more attractive character; and I'm sure that God loved Esau as much as he loves any human being. Yet God chose Jacob, despite Jacob's rotten behaviour (Genesis 25 and 27). This teaching is difficult to swallow, as Paul acknowledges. But he does not pull his punches! And while we wrestle with this teaching, it is worth remembering that Paul passionately wanted unbelieving Jews to become God's chosen people through Jesus. He did not say, 'God doesn't want them, so neither do I.'

14What are we to say, then? Is God guilty of injustice? Heaven forbid! 15For his words to Moses are – "I will take pity on whom I take pity, and be merciful to whom I am merciful." 16So, then, all depends, not on human wishes or human efforts, but on God's mercy. 17In scripture, again, it is said to Pharaoh – "It was for this purpose that I raised you to the throne, to show my power by my dealings with you, and to make my name known throughout the world." [18]So, then, where God wills, he takes pity, and where he wills, he hardens the heart. [19]Perhaps you will say to me – "How can anyone still be blamed? For who withstands his purpose?" [20]I might rather ask "Who are you who are arguing with God?" Does a thing which a person has moulded say to the person who has moulded it "Why did you make me like this?" [21]Has not the potter absolute power over their clay, so that out of the same lump they make one thing for better, and another for common, use?

THE QUESTION REMAINS, does God act fairly when he chooses to bless one person and not another, though they are both equally deserving? The point is that they are both equally undeserving. If God were to act purely with justice, none of us would receive mercy. But there is a further question: if God chooses not to save a person, can that person be blamed for continuing to sin? Isn't God choosing to allow them to sin, when he could have chosen to stop them? If God is loving, and salvation is by grace rather than merit, won't he save everyone eventually? These seem to me to be deeply philosophical questions, and I'm no philosopher. It seems to me to be parallel to a question all those who study human behaviour have to answer: if our behaviour is the result of our genes, our upbringing, and our historical and geographical environment – none of which we are responsible for – does that mean that we don't really have any freedom of choice? And if we don't have freedom of choice, how can we be held accountable for our behaviour? I'm sure there must be some philosophical answer which holds both sides of the coin together

– we do have free will and are responsible for our choices, and our choices could theoretically be predictable if all circumstances were known. So it is with the questions Paul is seeking to answer: we are responsible for our actions and will have to account for them some day, and God in his love chooses to save all who trust in him and in his Son Jesus. I cannot disentangle in my mind God's will and his knowledge of the future – how much does he choose what he knows will happen, and how much does what will happen depend on his choice? At this point I have to go along with Scripture: God knows everything that will happen, and he in sovereign love is working his purposes out through everything that happens.

As I reflect on these issues, I think of my own experience, mentioned in the Introduction. When I became aware of the necessity to accept Jesus as my Lord and my God, I felt unable to do so. I knew I was responsible for my choice to ignore Jesus' claims, I knew I was living a lie, but still could not bring myself to do otherwise. Then one evening, several months later, I felt that now was the time – I had to decide to accept Jesus, and did so. What was going on? I believe God enabled me to make that choice at that time, and not before; he made the choice to give me the power to decide to follow Jesus. Why then? Maybe that was the right time, for reasons unknown to me. It was God who saved me – yet I was fully responsible for the choice I made. In no way was I pressurised or forced to make it. My choice to accept Jesus as my Lord did not earn my salvation, but my salvation is a consequence of that choice.

Back to Paul's letter. He does not argue whether God is unjust or not – he simply says, 'Heaven forbid!' He accepts that God is righteous and incapable of injustice, without argument. And he accepts that God has the right to show pity and mercy to whichever undeserving sinner he chooses. There is hope for everyone! On the other hand, he also has the right to allow sinners to escape justice for a time – even for the rest of their lives – when there is good reason for it. Sometimes the reason is to give them time to repent (2 Peter 3:9). At other times, there is another purpose, as when God allowed Pharaoh to refuse to let his people Israel go free (Exodus chapters 6-14). God hardened Pharaoh's heart, as he has the right to. But we notice in those chapters of Exodus that Pharaoh first hardened his own heart; and God's hardening was simply saying 'so be it'. Quite often in Scripture we see that there is a time for making particular decisions; and if that time is not acted upon, it may pass – our hearts have become hardened, and we can no longer make the right choice.

In answer to the question, 'Who withstands God's purpose?' Paul responds, 'Who are you who are arguing with God?' Paul has a deep sense of God's majesty; he truly seeks God's honour and glory. However, it is possible to argue with God while seeking his glory: Paul here is answering people who are being cynical and unbelieving. It is often the case that people of faith can argue with God, and God can argue back! Sometimes it seems God even tries to provoke an argument, such as when he told Moses that he would destroy the unbelieving people of Israel and start again with him (Exodus 32:9-14). Paul uses the picture of a potter: the potter can make whatever he likes, and God our creator has the right to create whatever he likes. Paul is going to say that what God likes is always good and right; but the point he's making here is that God is God, the sovereign Lord, worthy of all our reverence and awe.

We often hear people complaining about the way God has made them or family members or friends – we compare ourselves with others and don't like what we see. Especially if there is some kind of disability – God, why? Paul's picture of the clay questioning the potter seems a harsh picture in these circumstances; yet the picture talks about things made for special purposes and things made for common use – both kinds are necessary for full life and have value. We probably won't know the answer to our complaints in this life; but we can be sure that one day we'll know what good things God had in mind when he made us, and we'll either praise him for it, or curse him to our immeasurable loss.

^{22}And what if God, intending to reveal his displeasure and make his power known, bore most patiently with the objects of his displeasure, though they were fit only to be destroyed, ^{23}so as to make known his surpassing glory in dealing with the objects of his mercy, whom he prepared beforehand for glory, ^{24}and whom he called – even us – not only from among the Jews but from among the Gentiles also! ^{25}This, indeed, is what he says in the book of Hosea – "Those who were not my people, I will call my people, and those who were unloved I will love. ^{26}And in the place where it was said to them – 'You are not my people', they will be called sons of the living God." ^{27}And Isaiah cries aloud over Israel – "Though the sons of Israel are like the sand of the sea in number, only a remnant of them will escape! ^{28}For the Lord will execute his sentence on the world, fully and without delay." ^{29}It is as Isaiah foretold – "Had not the Lord of Hosts spared some few of our people to us, we should have become like Sodom and been made to resemble Gomorrah."

'WHAT IF...' THIS SOUNDS to me as if Paul is speculating. But, being Paul, his speculations may be true! Those who oppose God and oppose the good news of Jesus, and all evil-doers, do indeed cause God displeasure, and the time will come when he will reveal that displeasure and give them what they deserve, with power and complete justice. However, that time has not yet come; he is 'bearing patiently' with them, allowing them to continue in their course of life. Why? Paul suggests that his purpose is to reveal his glory in the way he deals with us who have received mercy. How does his patience help? Paul does not explain at this point. But I think it may have something to do with the fact that the time for judgement on evil-doers is the time when Jesus returns to earth at the end of this age, in order to bring in the glories of the age to come. If God decided not to wait, and to bring in that time immediately, then that would not give time for the good news to spread over the world, and God's harvest would be very small. God's glory is revealed in his forgiveness and salvation for sinners; and he wants sinners from all over the world – Gentiles and Jews alike – to come to faith and repentance, and become his people, sons and daughters of the living God. The fact that not many of Paul's fellow Jews have accepted the salvation of Jesus was predicted by Isaiah hundreds of years before, when he said only a remnant would escape. Yet the few Jews who had accepted the good news of Jesus (including Paul himself) would prove vitally important to the spread of God's kingdom.

'Whom he prepared beforehand for glory'. This clause reflects the teaching that God chose his people from among the inhabitants of the world even before the earth existed (see Ephesians 1:4). We looked at this issue earlier in the chapter, asking how that could be fair, and how that affected our free will. The relationship between God's sovereign will and our free will is still something of a mystery to me. But I think the fairness aspect is more easily dealt with – grace is never fair, it is never deserved, and no-one has a right to receive unmerited favour. That said, I am not surprised that we feel bad about being the recipients of God's favour when others whom we admire and respect are not. When disasters happen, the survivors often ask, 'Why me?' and often feel guilty about their survival. Maybe this has something to do with being in solidarity with our fellow humans. Although believers in Jesus are a new creation in union with Christ, we are still living in this world, and it would be wrong for us to rejoice in the glories we now look forward to without caring about the troubles our fellow humans are suffering. And the whole of this section of Paul's letter is due to his discomfort in seeing his fellow Jews reject the good news.

[30]What are we to say, then? Why, that Gentiles, who were not in search of righteousness, secured it – a righteousness which was the result of faith; [31]while Israel, which was in search of a Law which would ensure righteousness, failed to discover one. [32]And why? Because they looked to obedience, and not to faith, to secure it. They stumbled over the stumbling-block. [33]As scripture says – "See, I place a stumbling-block in Zion

– a rock which will prove a hindrance; and he who believes in him will have no cause for shame.

PAUL NOW APPROACHES the heart of the problem of the Jewish rejection of Jesus. The solution to this problem will be revealed in a couple of chapters' time, but now he spells out the problem: we are judged righteous by God, not on the basis of obedience to God and his commands, but on the basis of our faith – faith in Jesus, as the next chapter makes clear. The Jews wanted to be right with God, but assumed that could only come through obedience to the Law of God. Paul has argued in this letter that obedience to the Law is impossible; righteousness has to come another way, and that way is through faith in Jesus which unites us with him so that we benefit from his bearing our sins on his cross, and his living a righteous life as our representative. Righteousness is a gift of God, it is grace; and that is a stumbling block to many people. They don't want charity, not even from God; they want the honour of do-it-yourself righteousness, which is an impossible dream. Those who believe in Jesus 'will have no cause for shame.' What a statement!

122

ROMANS CHAPTER 10

[1]My friends, my heart's desire and prayer to God for my people is for their salvation. [2]I can testify that they are zealous for the honour of God; but they are not guided by true insight, [3]for, in their ignorance of the divine righteousness, and in their eagerness to set up a righteousness of their own, they refused to accept with submission the divine righteousness. [4]For Christ has brought Law to an end, so that righteousness may be obtained by everyone who believes in him. [5]For Moses writes that, as for the righteousness which results from Law, those who practise it will find life through it. [6]But the righteousness which results from faith finds expression in these words: "Do not say to yourself 'Who will go up into heaven?'" (which means to bring Christ down) [7]"or 'Who will go down into the depths below?'" (which means to bring Christ up from the dead). [8]No, but what does it say? "The message is near you, on your lips and in your heart" (which means "The message of faith" which we proclaim). [9]For, if with your lips you acknowledge the truth of the message that JESUS IS LORD, and believe in your heart that God raised him

from the dead, you will be saved. [10]For with their hearts people believe and so attain to righteousness, while with their lips they make their profession of faith and so find salvation. [11]As the passage of scripture says – "No one who believes in him will have any cause for shame."

[12]For no distinction is made between the Jew and the Greek, for all have the same Lord, and he is bountiful to all who invoke him. [13]For everyone who invokes the name of the Lord will be saved.

Paul repeats his declaration of loving concern for his people. I notice that despite his firm belief in God's sovereign choice of whom to save, he still prays for his people to be saved – belief in God's sovereignty does not allow us to simply resign ourselves to what we think it means. Even when we think we know what God is doing in this or that bad situation, we don't just say, 'It's God's will.' We can still pray heartfelt prayer for a situation to change, however impossible it may seem.

Paul's Jewish opponents were indeed motivated by zeal for God's honour, as are many extremists today; but, as with those extremists, 'they are not guided by true insight.' They wanted to be right with God, but thought they could do it themselves – Paul talked about this in the earlier part of this letter. There he taught that our own righteousness can never measure up to God's standards. God's commands, his rules for life and worship, don't in themselves have any power to help us to keep them, and so we all fall short. The only way for us to be righteous in God's sight is for us to accept the offer of righteousness God gives us in Jesus. Paul's opponents – and, I suspect, the followers of most other religions then and now – cannot accept this, so they still seek to achieve fulfilment by their obedience to their religion's teaching. In the case of his Jewish opponents, they were right to believe that full obedience meant full acceptance by God; the difficulty was that full obedience is humanly impossible, which is why Jesus has opened a new way into life with God, a way that is accessible to all, of whatever race or creed.

The Scripture that Paul now quotes in verses 6-8 is not one I would have thought of! However, those of his readers who had been brought up in the Jewish faith would have known it well. It is taken from Deuteronomy 29:11-14, where Moses says that the commands of God he has passed on to the Israelites are not out of reach; they don't have to fetch them from heaven or from overseas in order to learn what to do, they already have them in their mouths and hearts – they are already talking about them and learning them. Paul in quoting them adds his own twist. Jesus is the one who teaches us what to do – he is the way, the truth and the life (John 14:6) – and he has already come from heaven to be born as a human being, and come back from as far away as it is possible to go, the depths of death, in order to be near us through the preaching and receiving of the gospel, the good news. The message of Jesus is 'on your lips and in your heart': with our lips we say, "Jesus is Lord', and we do so because we believe in our hearts that God raised him from the dead and has given him all authority in heaven and on earth. Our faith in Jesus unites us to him and to his righteousness; and that faith finds expression when we declare that Jesus is Lord. (Paul's words here may well reflect what went on when new believers were baptised. It may not always have been a public baptism; when Paul baptised the Philippian jailor and his household – Acts 16:33 – it was the middle of the night!)

To say "Jesus is Lord" meant a full commitment to him. "Caesar is Lord" was a declaration of submission to the Roman emperor; to say anyone else is Lord could be regarded as treason. The one who is our lord is the one we must obey above all other, even above ourselves! In Paul's day, and in many countries today, such a declaration of faith could well result in death; so belief in Jesus' resurrection, and in his promise that even if we die we have eternal life, was and is vital. The one who is our lord is not only the one we obey; he is also the one we can expect to help us – there is a two-way commitment. And whether Jew or Gentile, we have the same Lord, and he is ready to give us all the help we need – Jesus is the good shepherd, he is the one who saves us from trouble, from judgement and eternal death, for joy and everlasting life with him.

14But how, it may be asked, are they to invoke one in whom they have not learned to believe? And how are they to believe in one whose words they have not heard? And how are they to hear his words unless someone proclaims him? 15And how is anyone to proclaim him unless they are sent as his messengers? As scripture says – "How beautiful are the feet of those who bring good news!"

WHEREVER PAUL WENT on his missionary journeys, he always went to a synagogue or place of prayer to tell the good news of Jesus to his fellow Jews first, even though Jesus had called him to be an apostle to the Gentiles. The Jews, God's special people, needed to know that Jesus was their Messiah; but for that to happen they needed to know about him. (This translation talks about hearing Jesus' words; the original Greek translates literally as 'how shall they believe of whom they did not hear?', which most naturally means hearing about Jesus. However, if we want people to follow Jesus we have to tell them what he taught, as well as telling about his life and death and resurrection.) If the Jews needed to know about Jesus, then someone needed to tell them – and Paul says that person needs to have been sent as Jesus' messenger.

What does Paul mean? Who are Jesus' messengers? Paul quotes Isaiah to show what a beautiful thing it is to be one of Jesus' messengers, presenting the good news of freedom from sin and death. He himself knew that he had been sent by Jesus; and although he knew his ministry was particularly for those who were not Jews, he had to pass his message to the Jews first. He was an 'apostle', and that word is derived from a word meaning 'to send': all apostles were commissioned by Jesus to spread the good news. Another group of people similarly spreading the good news were 'evangelists'. (That word is derived from a word meaning 'good news'.) Paul includes evangelists among the list of people Christ has given to the church to build it up (along with apostles, prophets, pastors and teachers, Ephesians 4:11), and one of the seven people chosen to sort out problems in the early church in Acts 6 was Philip, who brought the good news of Jesus to Samaria (Acts 8) and was known as 'Philip the evangelist' (Acts 21:8). Paul told his colleague Timothy to 'do the work of an evangelist' (2 Timothy 4:5). But what about us? Are we sent by Jesus to pass on his good news? Or is that the task only of those who have received a definite commission from him, such as apostles and evangelists?

Many of us shrink from the task of spreading the good news. 'We don't know what to say!' 'We don't think our friends want to hear!' 'I don't want to be a Bible Basher!' These verses in Romans state clearly that we need to be sent (the word is the same as the one from which we get the word 'apostle'). We need to be commissioned. The 'great commission' in Matthew 28:16-20 was given to the eleven apostles who had been with Jesus from the time of his baptism by John, but they were told to make all nations his disciples, and that was a task they could only accomplish with the help of succeeding generations of Christians – it is a task for the whole church. Many argue that means that all Christians are commissioned to share the good news; but the 'great commission' was to go to all nations, and even in the early church not everyone became missionaries, nor was there any expectation that they should. They were told to be ready to explain their faith to those who asked them (1 Peter 3:16) – that is a sort of commissioning, and it is something we all can do. But if the good news of Jesus is to penetrate all over the world, it needs Christians to be ready to go wherever God sends them, and to share the good news whenever there is an opportunity to do so.

I believe that commissioning can take many forms. For some, like Paul, it comes as a definite call from the Lord. For others, it often begins with a desire implanted in our hearts for others to hear the good news and be saved. That has to be a heart desire, formed by love; if we spread the good news only out of a sense of duty, then we are in danger of serving our own needs rather than the needs of others. God may still use our words (e.g. Philippians 1:15-18), but I think that often the listeners can sense our wrong motives. If we want others to know (especially family and friends), God does give opportunities; and when those opportunities come, let's use them – say something! I don't think we need to worry too much about whether we are saying the right thing. It helps to have a good sense of what the good news is, but often we only have the opportunity to say a sentence or two – and God can use that, even if we're not sure we've said anything sensible! If the conversation develops, so much the better, but it does not always happen. I think all God requires is for us to open our mouths and speak when we sense he wants us to say something, and he will do the rest, putting thoughts into our minds, or words into our mouths, or maybe shutting us up when we've said all he wants us to say!

As I said earlier (in Chapter 1) I do not consider myself to be an evangelist. I have been on missions led by people who do have a gift of sharing the gospel both with individuals and with large crowds, and I have admired them greatly. On rare occasions I have taught about the good news and seen a surprising number of people respond (mostly in Uganda). At times I have thought about how best to present the good news of Jesus in as few words as possible – but have never had an occasion to use them! Mostly I believe I have simply been a link in a chain, and that my life or preaching or some conversations – or even the odd throw-away comment – have been used by God in drawing people to Jesus. It is a real privilege to be used by God in this way. I have come to the conclusion that there is no technique in evangelism. God works in his own sovereign way, and the way he works is as varied as the individuals he is working in. What he wants of us is a readiness to be partners with him in whatever situation he leads us into.

[16]Still, it may be said, everyone did not give heed to the good news. No, for Isaiah asks – "Lord, who has believed our teaching?" [17]And so we gather, faith is a

result of teaching, and the teaching comes in the message of Christ. [18]But I ask "Is it possible that people have never heard?" No, indeed, for – "Their voices spread through all the earth, and their message to the ends of the world." [19]But again I ask "Did not the people of Israel understand?" First there is Moses, who says – "I, the Lord, will stir you to rivalry with a nation which is no nation; against an undiscerning nation I will arouse your anger." [20]And Isaiah says boldly – "I was found by those who were not seeking me; I made myself known to those who were not inquiring of me." [21]But of the people of Israel he says – "All day long I have stretched out my hands to a people who disobey and contradict."

HEARING THE GOOD NEWS does not guarantee a good response. We may share the good news, believing we have done so at God's time and in God's way, but are met with doubts or negative reactions. That should not be a surprise. At other times our hearers believe us – our teaching is met with faith. There have to be words – faith cannot grow in a vacuum. And ultimately, the words are not ours, but are from the Holy Spirit; and the focus of the words is Jesus – the words are about him, not about us or our experiences (though those may illustrate the truths we're sharing).

Paul asks, 'Is it possible that people have never heard the good news?' He answers, 'No!' What was he thinking of? We know there are many people all over the world – even in our own country – who have never had the good news of Jesus shared with them in an appropriate way. Even in the Roman world of Paul's day, when the news of this new religious movement was being gossiped about almost everywhere, there must have been people who had never heard it – after all, one of the reasons Paul was writing to the Romans was to get support for preaching the gospel where Christ was not known, further west in Spain (Romans 15:20,28). So he cannot be using this quote in a mathematically exact way, as if everyone everywhere had heard the message; it must be a general point that the news about Jesus had already spread far and wide – the fact that it had already reached Rome was proof enough of that!

Why, then, had the message met with so much unbelief, especially from Paul's fellow Jews? Did they not understand it? Paul again quotes Scripture to make points he is about to elaborate on in the next chapter: that those the Jews despised – people who were not seeking God at all – would rouse their jealousy or anger; and that God was longing for reconciliation with his people, but they were turning away from him.

ROMANS CHAPTER 11

[1] I ask, then, "Has God rejected his people?" Heaven forbid! For I myself am an Israelite, a descendant of Abraham, of the tribe of Benjamin. [2] God has not rejected his people, whom he chose from the first. Have you forgotten the words of scripture in the story of Elijah – how he appeals to God against Israel? [3] "Lord, they have killed your prophets, they have pulled down your altars, and I only am left; and now they are eager to take my life." [4] But what was the divine response? "I have kept for myself seven thousand who have never bowed the knee to Baal." [5] And so in our own time, too, there is to be found a remnant of our nation selected by God in love. [6] But if in love, then it is not as a result of obedience. Otherwise love would cease to be love. [7] What follows from this? Why, that Israel as a nation failed to secure what it was seeking, while those whom God selected did secure it. [8] The rest grew callous; as scripture says – "God has given them a deadness of mind – eyes that are not to see and ears that are not to hear – and it is so to this very day." [9] David, too, says – "May their feasts prove a snare and a trap to them – a

hindrance and a retribution; [10]may their eyes be darkened, so that they cannot see; and do you always make their backs to bend."

We do not know what proportion of the Christians in Rome were Jewish. It is possible that as the number of Gentile believers grew they may have considered that God had now rejected the Jews, and Paul might have been aware of this danger and sought to correct such an idea – his teaching so far in this letter might be thought to add some weight to this. Whatever was going on, Paul strongly rejects the idea – 'Heaven forbid!'. Two facts support his case: first, that he himself was a Jew; and second, that throughout Jewish history, with all its rebelliousness, there had always been a minority who stayed faithful to God – a faithful 'remnant'. Paul emphasises that God's choice of the 'remnant' in his own day was made in love, not as a reward for obedience – all, like Paul, had been selected regardless of their former way of life. The blessings of the age to come were now promised to followers of Jesus, both Gentiles and the Jewish remnant, whereas the rest of the Jews had grown callous. Paul quotes Scripture (Isaiah 29:10 and Deuteronomy 29:4) to make the point that this callousness had often happened in history, and then quotes from a psalm of David that the early Christians took to refer to Jesus, Psalm 69:22-23. The words seem to imply that God is blinding the unbelievers, and punishing them for their refusal to believe; but I wonder if it is more that they reflect the power Jewish traditions and celebrations ('feasts') had to block the new message of Christ – the celebrations were so enjoyable that people did not want to give them up – and God is simply saying, 'Have it your own way.' In either case, that is not the end of the story.

¹¹I ask then – "Was their stumbling to result in their fall?" Heaven forbid! On the contrary, through their falling away salvation has reached the Gentiles, to stir the rivalry of Israel. ¹²And, if their falling away has enriched the world, and their failure has enriched the Gentiles, how much more will result from their full restoration!

PAUL HAS ALREADY SAID that God was behind what was going on – he was working his purposes out. The majority of Jews were refusing to accept the good news of Jesus; but that was a stumble, not a permanent fall. God's purpose was to set free his blessing from being focused on one race, so that it would be available to all. Paul hopes that seeing non-Jews being blessed would make the Jews want it too! The rejection of the message by the Jews had forced Paul to fulfil his calling by sharing it with the world everywhere he went, thereby bringing much more joy and blessing than if he had been confined to speaking to his own people; but he did not believe Jewish rejection would be for ever.

¹³But I am speaking to you who were Gentiles. ¹⁴Being myself an apostle to the Gentiles, I exalt my office, in the hope that I may stir my countrymen to rivalry, and so save some of them. ¹⁵For, if their being cast aside has meant the reconciliation of the world, what will their

reception mean, but life from the dead? [16]If the first handful of dough is holy, so is the whole mass, and if the root is holy, so are the branches. [17]Some, however, of the branches were broken off, and you, who were only a wild olive, were grafted in among them, and came to share with them the root which is the source of the richness of the cultivated olive. [18]Yet do not exult over the other branches. But, if you do exult over them, remember that you do not support the root, but that the root supports you. [19]But branches, you will say, were broken off, so that I might be grafted in. [20]True, it was because of their want of faith that they were broken off, and it is because of your faith that you are standing. Do not think too highly of yourself, but beware. [21]For, if God did not spare the natural branches, neither will he spare you. [22]See, then, both the goodness and the severity of God – his severity towards those who fell, and his goodness towards you, provided that you continue to confide in that goodness; otherwise you, also, will be cut off. [23]And they, too, if they do not continue in their unbelief, will be grafted in; for God has it in his power to graft them in again. [24]If you were cut off from your natural stock – a wild olive – and were grafted, contrary to the course of nature, on a good olive, much more will they – the natural branches – be grafted back into their parent tree.

PAUL WANTS THE GENTILES reading this letter to take note. He wants them to realise why he is so open in front of Jews about his commission to bring the good news of Jesus to them: it is because he hopes that at least some of the Jews will want what they see the Gentiles now have, and turn to Christ and be saved. The fact that God was working more among the Gentiles than among them means that God is reconciling all nations to himself, at least potentially. But Paul anticipates that the time will come when God will begin to work powerfully to bring salvation to his fellow Jews, and that will mean 'life from the dead'. But what does that mean? Surely it means more than eternal life for Jews too – that is implied by their reception by God. I think that when the Jews turn to their Messiah in great numbers, that will bring immense blessing to the whole world – it may even be the trigger that ushers in the return of Christ and the beginning of the new age, the age of resurrection life for the whole of creation. After all, the Jews were the first to be called God's people – they are the 'first handful of dough' from which the whole batch of dough, the 'root' from which all the branches, get their life as it were. Our present faith, our status as God's children, is founded upon the status and faith of the children of Israel.

Paul uses the analogy of grafting branches into a tree, a well-known technique used for olive trees and grapevines, among several other fruit trees. He pictures the cultivated olive tree as representing the people of God which, until Jesus, consisted of Jews and others who adopted their faith and traditions. Now that many Jews rejected Jesus, while many Gentiles accepted him as their Messiah, that can be pictured as natural branches being broken off the tree and wild branches being grafted in to partake of the nourishment and nature of the cultivated olive tree. The branches which have been grafted in – believing Gentiles – have no reason to think of themselves as superior to the natural branches which have been broken off. They remain in the olive tree only as long as they remain united to Jesus, trusting in him. The branches that were broken off had no faith in Jesus, and were therefore no longer God's people – and the same could happen to believing Gentiles if they ceased to believe. God is both good and severe – good to those who trust in him, severe to those who reject his Son. But if those Gentiles who trust turn away, or those Jews who have turned away change their minds and put their trust in Jesus, then the situation has changed – the wild branches will be removed, and the natural branches will be grafted back in again. It all depends on faith.

²⁵My friends, so that you don't think too highly of yourselves, I want you to recognise the truth, hitherto hidden, that the callousness which has come over Israel is only partial, and will continue only until the whole Gentile world has been gathered in. ²⁶And then all Israel will be saved. As scripture says – "From Zion will come the Deliverer; he will banish ungodliness from Jacob. ²⁷And they will see the fulfilment of my covenant, when I have taken away their sins." ²⁸From the standpoint of the good news, the Jews are God's enemies for your sake; but from the standpoint of God's selection, they are dear to him for the sake of the patriarchs. ²⁹For God never regrets his gifts or his call.

³⁰Just as you at one time were disobedient to him, but have now found mercy in the day of their disobedience;

³¹so, too, they have now become disobedient in your day of mercy, in order that they also in their turn may now find mercy. ³²For God has given all alike over to disobedience, that to all alike he may show mercy. ³³Oh! The unfathomable wisdom and knowledge of God! How inscrutable are his judgments, how untraceable his ways! Yes – ³⁴who has ever comprehended the mind of the Lord? Who has ever become his counsellor? ³⁵Or who has first given to him, so that he may claim a reward? ³⁶For all things are from him, through him, and for him. And to him be all glory for ever and ever! Amen.

PAUL NOW COMES TO THE point of all he has written in chapters 9 to 11. The unbelief of the Jews is only partial (for all the first disciples were Jews, and outside the Middle East there were still many like Paul who were believing Jews, as there are today); and it is only temporary. Paul has received revelation from God that the unbelief would 'continue only until the whole Gentile world has been gathered in'. That does not seem to me to imply that everyone in the world will believe in Jesus – Jesus taught that only a comparative few walk the narrow road to life, while the many are on the broad road to destruction (Matthew 7:13,14). 'The whole Gentile world' is literally 'the fullness of the nations', the full harvest from the world, from people of every nation, tribe, culture and religion. I believe there will come a time when the good news has run its course in the world, and those who are not Jews will no longer consider following Jesus. At that time the Jews will turn to him. 'And then all Israel will be saved' – all the spiritual descendants of Abraham. That mass turning to Christ among the Jews will be the fulfilment of many Old Testament prophecies. After all, they are still deeply beloved by God, despite their present enmity to Jesus and his followers, and God who called them to be his people has not changed his mind about them, he is merely waiting for the right time. They are being disobedient now, refusing to live by faith in Jesus, while the Gentile believers have received grace and forgiveness; but in due time many if not all unbelieving Jews will also receive grace and forgiveness and follow Jesus. This, at least, is my interpretation of what Paul wrote; I may of course be wrong!

Paul recognises that all this is rather mysterious. But instead of being unhappy about it, he rejoices! God's wisdom and knowledge are unfathomable – we can never plumb their depths. We cannot expect to understand all God's ways and activity – God is much too great for that – and that is a cause for joy and praise! We don't have a handmade god! No human can tell God what to do, as if he didn't know. No human being has put God in their debt. All things in this world are 'from him', and have their origin in him, the world's creator; every natural process is directed 'through him', the world's sustainer; and everything is 'for him', for his honour and glory and pleasure. So Paul concludes this portion of his letter, 'To him be glory for ever and ever! Amen.'

ROMANS CHAPTER 12

¹I entreat you, then, friends, by the mercies of God, to offer your bodies as a living and holy sacrifice, acceptable to God, for this is your rational worship. ²Do not conform to the fashion of this world; but be transformed by the complete change that has come over your minds, so that you may discern what God's will is – all that is good, acceptable, and perfect.

U p until now, Paul has been teaching that we have been united with Christ through our faith in him and commitment to him, a commitment expressed in our baptism and affirmed by the Holy Spirit's presence in us. Whether Jew or Gentile, we who believe are the people of God; more, we are God's children. In chapters 9 to 11 he looked at how those who have been God's special people – the Jews – now stand in relationship with God when as a whole they reject Jesus as their Messiah and are not united with him. He ended that portion with the illustration of an olive tree, with branches united to the roots either naturally or through grafting. Now he turns to consider how all this teaching affects our daily lives.

Paul gives many instructions in this part of his letter. It is tempting to give these instructions the status of law – the law of Christ, as it were. But Paul has declared that we have died to the law through our union with Christ in his death, and cannot be condemned for our shortcomings. So I believe these instructions are simply Paul unpacking what the fullness of life in union with Christ looks like – this is how Christ in us wants to live through our minds and bodies.

Verse 1 sets the tone. Paul has the authority of an apostle to issue commands; instead he entreats us. The reason for his entreaty is God's loving mercy and grace that he has been unfolding in this letter; and the natural, rational, response is to 'offer our bodies as a living and holy sacrifice'. If we are spiritually united with Christ, that is bound to affect what we do with our hands and tongues and eyes and feet – Christ's Spirit lives in us, and he is our Lord! The negative side of this is that Christians must not let what everyone else thinks O.K. guide us – 'Do not let the world squeeze you into its mould', as J. B. Phillips translates it. Instead, we are to focus on the positive side: we are a new creation with new life (Christ's resurrection life), we have a new relationship with God (through the Holy Spirit living in us), and we have a new destination (the age to come), What goes on in our minds is vitally important. We still have our old memories, and our old natural desires (often selfish); but we also have in our minds the story and teaching of Jesus and his apostles, and the new desires to do what God wants and to become more and more like Jesus. Our minds have been renewed, and are continuing to be renewed as we grow in our knowledge of God and our experience of life with him. We are increasingly able to discern his will in all our situations and experiences, and to see how good, acceptable and perfect that will is. God is love!

God has given us freedom of choice. We can choose whether or not to align ourselves with his will. That is why Paul entreats us to offer our bodies deliberately to him, giving up our right to self-determination in order to become the people God wants us to be. It often feels like a sacrifice – we are sacrificing ourselves. But it is the only reasonable response to God's sacrifice for us that we might truly be his beloved children, working with him for the salvation of the world and the growth of his kingdom. Paul in chapter 6:13 said, 'Do not offer any part of your bodies to sin, in the cause of unrighteousness, but once for all offer yourselves to God (as those who, though once dead, now have life), and devote every part of your bodies to the cause of righteousness.' That is a 'once for all' decision, a fork in the road, followed by a continual giving of every part of our bodies to good action – we give our brains (what we imagine, what we dwell on), our words, what we look at and the way we look at them, what we do. As Paul said to the Colossians, 'Whatever you say or do, do everything in the name of the Lord Jesus; and through him offer thanksgiving to God the father' (Colossians 3:17).

³In fulfilment of the charge with which I have been entrusted, I tell every one of you not to think more highly of themselves than they ought to think, but to think until they learn to think soberly – in accordance with the measure of faith that God has allotted to each.

⁴For, just as in the human body there is a union of many parts, and each part has its own function, ⁵so we, by our union in Christ, many though we are, form but one body, and individually we are related one to another as its parts. ⁶Since our gifts differ in accordance with

the particular charge entrusted to us, if our gift is to preach, let our preaching correspond to our faith; [7]if it is to minister to others, let us devote ourselves to our ministry; the teacher to their teaching, [8]the counsellor to their counsel. Let the person who gives in charity do so with a generous heart; let the person who is in authority exercise due diligence; let the person who shows kindness do so in a cheerful spirit.

PAUL WAS COMMISSIONED by the Lord to be an apostle to the Gentiles, proclaiming to them the good news that God was in Christ reconciling the world, not just the Jews, to himself, and that if they turned from their sins, put their trust in Jesus and learned to follow him they would be saved from condemnation by God and given a place in the glorious world to come. I would expect him, in fulfilment of that charge, to write something more about faith or righteousness, or repentance from some of the sins mentioned in chapter 1. But Paul, to my surprise, before saying anything else about how to live as followers of Christ, tells his readers not to think too highly of themselves. Why? Why is that of first importance?

I suspect that what Paul is dealing with is the sin of pride which, after all, underlies so much of the evil in the world – and is a sin that Christians are often accused of. Not all pride is sin; Paul himself is happy to boast – but not about his achievements, more about his weaknesses. The problem comes when we think ourselves better than someone else and look down on them. It may be that Gentile believers were being tempted to look down on Jewish believers, or that one race or class looked down on others – history is full of such cases. But we are all equal in the sight of God.

Paul goes on to talk about life within the Christian community with respect to the gifts God gives us with which to serve him. He uses the illustration of the human body, an illustration he also uses in his first letter to the Corinthians (chapter 12). Each part of the body has a different function; likewise each believer is given some gift or other with which to serve Jesus and build up the whole. We are united to Christ, and therefore to each other. Paul in his letter to the Corinthians states that some gifts are more useful in building up the body than others, and tells them to seek those kinds of gifts. But the fact that some gifts are more visible or useful than others is not an excuse for pride – they are gifts, nor rewards, and the fact that one gift has been given to one person in particular circumstances does not mean they are better than someone with another gift given in different circumstances – each part of the body needs to work in harmony with the rest of the body, in which we are united together.

Paul tells his readers to think of themselves in accordance with the measure of faith that God has allotted to each. How is faith measured? I don't think Paul is thinking how much we trust Jesus for salvation. He is talking about the gifts God gives each one of us, and each gift can only be exercised in faith – faith in God's power to accomplish his purpose in giving us that gift. We are to think of ourselves in proportion to our faith in God's power, not our own. Some gifts obviously require a lot of faith; others seem to be easy, especially if they coincide with our natural talents. But the latter require as much faith as the former if they are truly to build up Christ's kingdom. The faith that God allots to us is sufficient for his purposes; if someone is a successful evangelist, used by God to bring many to faith, God will have given them a great measure of faith in the power of the gospel. Someone whose gift is to help others in practical ways will have been given enough faith to bring glory and pleasure to God in those tasks. Both have been given faith in God; they could do nothing by themselves, they are totally dependent on God. Sometimes when I hear a famous evangelist I think that I could preach just as good a message; but I could only do that with God's power, and he has called me to work for him in a different field. There is simply no reason for pride in anything we think of as our achievements – the achievement is God's, not ours, and all the glory should go to him.

Whatever our gifts, we are to devote ourselves to using them in a godly way. It is interesting what gifts Paul mentions – not just preaching ('prophecy' is the word Paul uses, which is the gift of hearing and passing on a message from God), or serving the church in practical ways ('ministering'), or teaching God's truth; but also counselling ('exhorting'), charitable giving, leadership, acts of kindness. Generosity and cheerfulness are important – all too often I don't feel very cheerful when serving God and his people, especially when the task God has given me is not one I would choose to do! This reminds me to make sure that my attitude is right; it is the Lord Christ I am serving, and it is a privilege to do so, however menial or boring or difficult or unappreciated the task.

⁹Let your love be sincere. Hate the wrong; cling to the right. ¹⁰In the love of the community of the Lord's followers, be affectionate to one another; in showing respect, set an example of deference to one another; ¹¹never flagging in zeal; fervent in spirit; serving the

Master; [12]rejoicing in your hope; steadfast under persecution; persevering in prayer; [13]relieving the wants of Christ's people; devoted to hospitality. [14]Bless your persecutors – bless and never curse. [15]Rejoice with those who are rejoicing, and weep with those who are weeping. [16]Let the same spirit of sympathy animate you all, not a spirit of pride; enjoy the company of ordinary people. Do not think too highly of yourselves.

PAUL LISTS A WHOLE lot of aspects of new creation life as we follow Jesus. He does not say much about each one; but what a description they are of the Christian life! This is what we are aiming at! So I need to take a closer look at each item on Paul's list.

'Let your love be sincere.' How? I'm quite good (I think) at being polite to people at church, but I'm well aware of Jesus' command to love one another as he loves us, and politeness is not quite the same thing as love! Perhaps the emphasis should be on sincerity – Paul does not want Christians to act as if they loved a fellow Christian, when in their hearts they are looking down or disrespecting them. Part of my difficulty may be my expectations of what love involves – especially when it comes to memory: if I loved a person, shouldn't I remember not only their names, but also details of their lives they have previously shared? Some people are brilliant at that, and I admire them greatly – it is so affirming when someone remembers such things, and those at the receiving end feel they matter. But my memory lets me down – it always has! At school I could never remember history dates, and learning a language has always been difficult because of the need to learn vocabulary – constant repetition helps, and there are some things that really do stick in my mind. Is a good memory necessary for sincere love? Surely not! So my recipe for sincere love is first, to see the person I am with as someone who is deeply loved by God and by Christ in me; then, to give them my full attention (that's something I need to learn to do better); then, to care about them and about what they're telling me, as Jesus in me cares (that, too, is something I don't always find easy); then, if action is required, to do what I can and to do it cheerfully – but not to attempt what is impossible for me, and not to do something I can do if it would be better for someone else to do it. I still have a lot to learn!

'Hate the wrong, cling to the right.' Sincere love goes hand in hand with hating evil, whether it is the evil of a natural disaster, or the evil of wrong-doing. Tolerance is not love. Patient endurance may be necessary when the evil cannot be escaped; but we can continue to hate what we are enduring! However, hating the wrong does not mean we hate the wrong-doer – Jesus told us to love our enemies, and there are times when love for a wrong-doer has to insist on justice being done, however painful it may be to say so. When we punish one of our children for a misdeed, that does not mean we love them the less – nor does God's discipline detract from his love. 'Cling to the right', to what is good. 'For we are God's handiwork, created, by our union with Christ Jesus, for the good actions in doing which God had pre-arranged that we should spend our lives' (Ephesians 2:10). We are created to do good! But it needs effort to cling to what is good, for at times we really don't feel like it, and put it off or forget about it.

'Be affectionate to one another.' (The previous phrase, 'In the community of the Lord's followers', is a brave attempt to translate a word often rendered as 'in brotherly love'.) Again the question is, 'How?' For many of us, affection is often shown by touch; yet there are many others who don't like to be touched (depending on the circumstances). I guess that if we know the other person well enough we can act in accordance with their preferences; if not, withhold the touch and be affectionate through looks! We need always to avoid any touch or look that the recipient may feel uncomfortable with. This leads straight away to the next clause:

'In showing respect, set an example of deference to one another.' This ties in with Paul's instructions in Philippians 2:4: 'In humility lift others up above yourselves, considering not only your own interests but also the interests of others.' This requires grace on our part – 'undeserved love' – for we may be tempted to feel that the person we are with is below us in spirituality, education, class or whatever, so they do not merit deference! Nothing could be further from the truth: our Lord Jesus puts them on exactly the same level as us (and us on the same level as them), and his Spirit is in us both. (That is why Philippians 2 goes on in the famous passage of vs 5-10.) Paul will say more about this in verse 16.

Be 'never flagging in zeal; fervent in spirit; serving the Master.' Now that I am in my 70's, I find I do flag! I think it is right to be sensible and to try not to do too much, for I pay for it later – much of the Christian race is a marathon, not a sprint. But my zeal and my fervency need not flag, even when my physical and mental abilities are. The important thing is the last phrase, 'serving the Master.' When I think 'Oh no, I've got to do such and such', it really helps to think again, 'But I'm doing it for Christ.' If I can't do it for Christ, I shouldn't be doing it. This applies to everything we do in our daily lives. Paul told slaves in his day to serve their masters well, even if they were bad masters, because they were really serving Jesus and would be rewarded for their service to him in due course. (See Colossians 3:22-25.)

'Rejoicing in your hope' – in the future God has promised us. We don't know the details; so hope is not the same as knowledge, and is very much related to faith: we trust God to keep his promises, and we are absolutely certain that, as Paul reminded the Corinthians, 'What eye never saw, nor ear ever heard, what never entered people's minds – all these things God has prepared for those who love him' (1 Corinthians 2:9). Peter says more: 'Blessed is the God and Father of our Lord Jesus Christ, who has, in his great mercy, through the resurrection of Jesus Christ from the dead, given us the new life of undying hope, that promises an inheritance, imperishable, stainless, unfading, which has been reserved for you in heaven – for you who, through faith, are being guarded by the power of God, awaiting a salvation that is ready to be revealed in the last days. At the thought of this you are full of exultation, though (if it has been necessary) you have suffered for the moment somewhat from various trials' (1 Peter 1:3-6). We can rejoice in our hope even when our present circumstances are horrendous. I admit I find it difficult to overflow with joy when I can't imagine what the future God has prepared for us will be like. Maybe there's some truth in the old saying, 'Happiness happens, but joy abides.' But the thought strikes me that our joy in our hope is not so much because of what exactly God has planned for us, but because of Who is doing the planning – our loving heavenly Father, together with our Lord and Saviour Jesus Christ. Joy in hope is intimately related to joy in the Lord!

'Steadfast under persecution.' The word translated 'persecution' means more than that – it is pressure, affliction of any sort. (We could call it persecution from the devil, however it happens.) Paul prayed for the Colossians that they may be 'made strong at all points with a strength worthy of the power manifested in his glory – strong to endure with patience, and even with gladness, whatever may happen' (Colossians 1:11). Our power to endure comes from God; and I'm sure that knowing he has a glorious future planned for us can help! I'm also sure that such endurance is not mere survival, but includes continuing to try to be Christ-like in these circumstances – with the help of his Spirit within us.

'Persevering in prayer.' Paul doesn't say what he expects the prayer to be about; just that he wants his readers to keep lines of communication with God open under all circumstances. There are times when we feel prayer is impossible, especially when suffering depression; yet 'My God, my God, why have you forsaken me?' is a prayer, good enough for Jesus on the cross.

'Relieving the wants of God's people.' Jesus commands his people, 'love one another as I have loved you' (John 13:34), and James reminds us that such love needs to be practical, helping those in need (see James 2:14-17). We are to be charitable people, helping regardless of creed, culture, etc. (loving our neighbour), but especially, Jesus says, helping needy Christian brothers and sisters. Matthew 25:31-46, Jesus' parable of the sheep and the goats, makes this point very strongly; helping any needy Christian is helping Jesus himself. We are united to Jesus and his Spirit is in each one of us. When Paul wrote this letter he was on his way to Jerusalem with money collected on his travels to help needy Christians there (Romans 15:25) – he put his own teaching into practice. He did not live in a democracy, and had no political influence. But we are able to be charitable people in more ways than simply giving our time and resources. So often what is needed is not just 'charity', but social or political action – and we are able to do that, and do it not just for our Christian neighbours. Jesus came to this world to be the means of its salvation through his death and resurrection; however, he spent three years (probably) going about healing people as well as teaching them, regardless of whether they were deserving or not. Our actions to relieve poverty or distress will, I believe, not only be rewarded by God in due course, but will also in some way contribute towards God's mission to bring his kingdom to full perfection – a perfection we will only see when Jesus comes again, when the new creation is revealed in all its glory, and poverty and tears are no more.

'Devoted to hospitality.' The word translated 'hospitality' means literally 'fondness of strangers', and that meant treating strangers as guests and providing them with lodging, food and friendship. Frances and I experienced Middle Eastern hospitality on a trip to the Holy Land. I got talking to some men mending a wall, and one of them offered to take us on a walk down the Wadi Qelt to Jericho. We accepted, and it was a great experience. Afterwards he took us in a taxi to his home, where we found his wife had prepared a sumptuous meal for us – total strangers! And in Nazareth when we went for a walk a man sitting in his garden hailed us and invited us up for a cup of tea! In our culture we are taught to be wary of strangers. We do have a 'hospitality industry' in the U.K.; but shouldn't we who are Christians be more hospitable? Especially to other Christians? Does it really matter if our home is not as tidy as it would be if we were expecting guests?

'Bless your persecutors – bless and never curse.' Many Christians all over the world are suffering severe persecution, and those in 'safe countries' cannot assume persecution will never reach them. The greatest blessing a persecutor would have would be the blessing of repentance and faith in Jesus; but we can also pray for their well-being, however much our earthly nature cries out for vengeance. We may cry to the Lord for justice, but if we are blessing our persecutors we cannot at the same time wish them harm – despite the feelings expressed in many of the Psalms. Paul in this instruction is echoing Jesus' teaching in the sermon on the mount in Matthew 5:10-12, 43-46.

'Rejoice with those who are rejoicing, and weep with those who are weeping.' This requires us to lay aside our own concerns in order to feel for those who are rejoicing or weeping – not very easy! But what a difference it makes when we do this! We may find that we are not always on the receiving end of such empathy – some people can be very insensitive to how we are feeling, and we may then feel we do not matter to them. If that happens, that should teach us not to do the same!

'Let the same spirit of sympathy animate you all, not a spirit of pride; enjoy the company of ordinary people. Do not think too highly of yourselves.' Paul is reiterating what he said in v. 10, and earlier in chapter 12 – it is important. It is what Jesus did, and his Spirit lives in us. The most 'ordinary' people have much to teach us, and have skills we can respect. When I was teaching in a simple Bible College in Uganda some of my students had very little education. But they all knew how to live in times when they had no money, they could build their own houses and grow their own food; and they all spoke at least some English and some other languages as well. In all these respects they were above me, their teacher!

¹⁷Never return injury for injury. Aim at doing what everyone will recognise as honourable. ¹⁸If it is possible,

as far as rests with you, live peaceably with everyone.

[19]Never avenge yourselves, dear friends, but make way for the wrath of God; for scripture declares – "'It is for me to avenge, I will requite,' says the Lord." [20]Rather – "If your enemy is hungry, feed him; if he is thirsty, give him to drink. By doing this you will heap coals of fire on his head." [21]Never be conquered by evil, but conquer evil with good.

IN SOME CULTURES, TAKING revenge for an injury is thought of as an honourable thing to do. But if we seek revenge, it is difficult to make it an exact repayment for the injury, so the result may well be a spiralling feud. Paul's word for 'injury' is literally 'evil'; if anyone does something bad to us, he tells us not to do anything bad back – it is never honourable to do evil. So Jesus taught us not to seek revenge but to 'turn the other cheek' (Matthew 5:39). God is the giver of peace; he wants the world to be a world of peace, and his people are to be an example to all. But just as it takes two people to make a quarrel, so true peace needs both parties to be reconciled, and that is not always possible – even if we want peace, the others may not. In that case, we will not be held responsible for the lack of peace.

Paul reiterates the need to avoid vengeance. Ultimately, justice is God's domain. Even when we rightfully seek for justice it may not always be done here on earth; but we can be sure that God will do the right thing eventually, even if the judgement has to wait until Jesus returns. 'If your enemy is hungry, feed him; if he is thirsty, give him to drink. By so doing you will heap coals of fire on his head.' Paul is quoting from Proverbs 25:22, which adds, 'and the

Lord will reward you.' But what are these 'coals of fire'? Scholars are divided between those who think that our kindness will encourage our enemies to repent – the coals of fire are coals of shame; and those who think that our kindness will add to their sentence if they do not repent – the coals of fire are coals of punishment. It could well be that both are meant. Whatever lies behind it, the final sentence in this chapter sums up Paul's teaching on this subject: 'Never be conquered by evil, but conquer evil with good.' If we seek revenge, or hold hatred or bitterness in our hearts, we are being conquered by evil; if we do good to those who hate us or hurt us, the good will win – maybe not immediately, but in the long run. Jesus told us to forgive those who sin against us, just as we want to be forgiven by God; and his parable of the unforgiving servant (Matthew 18:21-35) is a stark warning that we cannot expect to be forgiven if we in turn do not forgive others.

'Conquer evil with good.' That is what God is doing all the time. People complain when God does not immediately punish those who do evil – he does not even force them to stop. Paul in Ephesians 6 reminds us that we are not fighting against flesh and blood but against spiritual opposition; behind all evil-doing and evil circumstances are the devil and all his wicked forces, who seek to undo all that God is doing in order to turn people against him. If we respond to evil with good, the devil has lost that battle; and when the devil does his worst and good people do not give in to evil – even if it results in their death – there's nothing more he can do. We see this at the cross of Jesus. The time will come when all evil will be dealt with; and the good we do in response to evil surely plays a part in winning the ultimate victory. 'Amid all these things we more than conquer through him who loved us!'

ROMANS CHAPTER 13

[1]Let everyone obey the supreme authorities. For no authority exists except by the will of God, and the existing authorities have been appointed by God. [2]Therefore the one who sets themself against the authorities is resisting God's appointment, and those who resist will bring a judgement on themselves. [3]A good action has nothing to fear from rulers; a bad action has. Do you want to have no reason to fear the authorities? Then do what is good, and you will win their praise. [4]For they are God's servants appointed for your good. But, if you do what is wrong, you may well be afraid; for the sword they carry is not without meaning! They are God's servants to inflict his punishments on those who do wrong. [5]You are bound, therefore, to obey, not only through fear of God's punishments, but also as a matter of conscience. [6]This, too, is the reason for your paying taxes; for the officials are God's officers, devoting themselves to this special work. [7]In all cases pay what is due from you – tribute where tribute is due, taxes where taxes are due, respect where respect is due, and honour where honour is due.

When Paul wrote this letter to the Romans, it was one continuous piece of prose – no verses, no chapters, it all flowed together. So these instructions about our relationship to authority follow immediately after the last words of chapter 12: 'Conquer evil with love'! If this letter was written around 57 AD, which seems likely, the emperor in Rome would have been Nero (54-68 AD), whose policies in the early years of his reign were generally well received; but Paul knew as well as anyone that Roman officials could be bad as well as good. So when he wrote this instruction to obey the supreme authorities he would have had no illusions about their merits, and his reason for insisting upon obedience was his belief that God is the supreme ruler of the world and that earthly rulers are in position because of God's will, not because they deserve it.

Paul was well aware of the history of Israel as recorded in the Scriptures. David was one of the heroes of the story – the shepherd boy who killed the giant Goliath and became king of Israel after the first king, Saul, had been killed in battle, was 'a man after God's own heart'; but when Saul wanted to kill him and tried to hunt him down, David kept in mind that Saul had been anointed king by God and refused to try to harm him. David had good reason to resist Saul, but did not rebel; David did what was right, yet Saul nevertheless wanted him dead. Paul knew this, but still wrote, 'A good action has nothing to fear from rulers.' Maybe he had heard of Jesus' words, later recorded in Luke 12:4: ' Do not be afraid of those who kill the body, but after that can do no more.' Ultimately, God works all things together for good for those who love him; so as long as we keep doing good, we need not fear the consequences even if they lead to our death from wicked authorities. As we saw at the end of Chapter 12, good will conquer evil; and in the end, good actions will win praise from authorities when they come to see that what was done was for the best.

I saw this during our time in Uganda. Where we were living was for a while controlled by rebels during a civil war. The government sent three ministers to try to negotiate peace with rebel leaders. They first met with some church ministers, and I and a colleague were among them. I suggested they met rebel leaders in rebel territory rather than in territory controlled by the army. They agreed, and a few days later my colleague and I took them to meet the leaders. The rebels then abducted them! Some in the government thought we were to blame; but when we were taken to see the army commander in the region he recognised that we were trying to promote peace, and acquitted us from all blame – much to our relief!

Paul supported the rule of law in civic affairs. God has delegated to human government the work of punishing evil, and even if officials are corrupt they are entitled to respect purely on account of their positions. Christians should be notable for being good citizens, taking an active part in the life and affairs of their communities, and happy to be involved in all walks of life including politics, as the Lord leads. Governments need money to do their work; we all, even if we are being discriminated against, have a duty to pay the taxes that are demanded. If officials do wrong, they are accountable to God who will in due course give them what they deserve. We may well disagree with their decisions, and accuse them of wrong-doing; but even so, we are to treat them with respect. In a democracy, that is not to say we should only vote for the government in power – elections are one way God uses to make his appointments. Opposition politicians are also worthy of respect! And the more followers of Jesus who get involved in politics, the better! I don't think that should lead to a so-called 'theocratic' government; when Jesus comes again that is what will happen, for at his name every knee will bow, but until then governments will be human institutions, led by fallible human beings, and the idea of putting religious leaders at the helm of government is most likely in my view to give their religion a bad name. Much wrong has been done by leaders claiming to be led by God.

Is there ever a case for resisting authorities appointed by God? Is civil disobedience ever justified? Yes. It happened in the early church when Peter and John were brought before the rulers of the Jews and were told to stop preaching about Jesus. They replied, 'Whether it is right, in the sight of God, to listen to you rather than to him – judge for yourselves, for we cannot help speaking of what we have seen and heard' (Acts 4:19-20). There are cases in the Old Testament where resistance had God's approval. When Israel broke up, and ten tribes declared independence from the Jerusalem regime, the surviving two were told by a prophet not to try to force them back into union, because this was God's doing (see 1 Kings 12:24). And when the wicked queen Athaliah was dethroned by force and killed (2 Kings 11), that story is told with approval, for it restored descendants of King David to the throne in line with God's promises. Resistance to wicked regimes may be the right thing to do; but I believe such courses of action should only be undertaken in extreme circumstances, with minimal use of force, and after much prayer.

^{8}Owe nothing to anyone except love; for they who love their neighbour have satisfied the Law. ^{9}The commandments, "You must not commit adultery, you must not kill, you must not steal, you must not covet," and whatever other commandment there is, are all summed up in the words – "You must love your neighbour as you love yourself." ^{10}Love never wrongs a neighbour. Therefore love fully satisfies the Law.

IN PAUL'S WORLD DEBT was generally a bad thing. In the Western world of today debt is regarded as a necessity – in the UK, university undergraduates amass a very large debt to pay for their courses, unless they or their parents are rich enough to pay the course fees themselves. Buying a car or a house is so expensive that most people need to get finance to pay for them, and some people accrue so much debt that they are unable to pay off the interest, and the debt grows. In many places in Paul's day inability to pay off a debt could result in being sold as a slave – Jesus' parable of the unforgiving servant (Matthew 18) included that possibility. Luke's version of the Lord's prayer includes the clause, 'for we ourselves forgive everyone who wrongs us' (Luke 11:4) and the word 'wrongs us' is more literally 'is in debt to us'. So Paul encourages debt-free living – except for the debt of love that we owe to God, our neighbours, and especially fellow followers of Jesus. For some of us, that seems an impossible request; but organisations like 'Christians Against Poverty' do a great job in helping people to come out of debt. Let's support them!

Jesus stated that the second most important command of God after the command to love him with all our heart is the command to love our neighbour as we love ourselves (from Leviticus 19:18). Jesus said that the whole of the law and the prophets (in other words, all their Scriptures) depended on those two laws. Paul echoes this – love fully satisfies the law, for the law was designed to help people live with God and each other, punishing wrong-doing. Such laws (Paul is talking about religious laws) are unnecessary where love reigns and God's laws are written on our hearts.

[11]This I say, because you know the crisis that we have reached, for the time has already come for you to rouse yourselves from sleep; our salvation is nearer now than when we accepted the faith. [12]The night is almost gone; the day is near. Therefore let us be done with the deeds of darkness, and arm ourselves with the weapons of light. [13]Being in the light of day, let us live becomingly, not in revelry and drunkenness, not in lust and licentiousness, not in quarrelling and jealousy. [14]No! Arm yourselves with the spirit of the Lord Jesus Christ, and spend no thought on your earthly nature, to satisfy its cravings.

WHY WAS IT SO IMPORTANT to Paul to emphasise this teaching about love conquering evil in all its forms? He says it is because of the crisis he and his readers were facing. I don't know exactly what he had in mind; the persecution of Christians under Nero and the Jewish revolt against Roman rule were still a few years in the future; maybe there were stirrings which Christians recognised – their faith was not yet acceptable anywhere, and they were regarded with suspicion by Jews and Gentiles alike. Jesus had foretold days of great trial before he would return, and Paul seems to think all this was about to happen – the day of Jesus' return was certainly closer and closer as time went on. For us it is closer still! But persecution and trials have been a feature for Christians throughout history (and sadly Christians have often been the persecutors) – the greatest amount of persecution has occurred in the last century or so. How should we respond? With resistance to authorities? With vengeance? Do we give in and renounce our faith or the way of life Jesus taught? These are all deeds of darkness, and Paul has warned us not to be conquered by evil in this way, but to conquer evil with good. How?

Paul gives us a positive action and a negative one. The positive one is to 'arm yourselves with the spirit of the Lord Jesus Christ'. In Ephesians 6 he elaborates this, using Roman armour as a visual aid – as a soldier puts on his armour, so we put on truth, righteousness, a readiness to share the good news of Jesus, faith, salvation, the word of God, and prayer in the Spirit. The Holy Spirit whom God has given us lives in us, and is stronger than any evil foe, so it makes sense to trust him and his guidance more than any other resources we may be tempted to use by ourselves.

The negative action is simply to avoid even thinking about how we could satisfy our earthly desires. I find that easier said than done. Often when I hear of difficult or dangerous events in the news, or of some wrong being done, or some very attractive event, my imagination gets to work in a big way and I imagine what I might do in that situation – and often I catch myself thinking in a very 'earthly' way, not according to the Spirit. However, earthly desires tend to fade away if we simply neglect them.

ROMANS CHAPTER 14

¹As for those whose faith is weak, always receive them as friends, but not for the purpose of passing judgement on their scruples. ²One person's faith permits them to eat food of all kinds, while another whose faith is weak eats only vegetable food. ³The person who eats meat must not despise the person who abstains from it; nor must the person who abstains from eating meat pass judgement on the one who eats it, for God himself has received them. ⁴Who are you, that you should pass judgement on the servant of another? Their standing or falling concerns their own master. And stand they will, for their Master can enable them to stand. ⁵Again, one person considers some days to be more sacred than others, while another considers all days to be alike. Everyone ought to be fully convinced in their own mind. ⁶The person who observes a day, observes it to the Master's honour. They, again, who eat meat eat it to the Master's honour, for they give thanks to God; while the person who abstains from it abstains from it to the Master's honour, and also gives thanks to God. ⁷There is not one of us whose life concerns ourselves

alone, and not one of us whose death concerns ourself alone; [8]for, if we live, our life is for the Master, and, if we die, our death is for the Master. Whether, then, we live or die we belong to the Master. [9]The purpose for which Christ died and came back to life was this – that he might be Lord over both the dead and the living. [10]I would ask the one "Why do you judge other followers of the Lord?" And I would ask the other "Why do you despise them?" For we will all stand before the court of God. [11]For scripture says – "'As surely as I live,' says the Lord, 'every knee will bend before me and every tongue will praise God.'" [12]So, then, each one of us will have to render account of himself to God.

Paul now turns his attention back to life within the Christian community. When Jesus commanded us to love one another, he was well aware that his followers would come from all walks of life and have very different backgrounds and views, which would not be easy to weld together. This diversity came into sharp focus when the good news started to gain ground in the non-Jewish world of the Roman empire, when people who had been used to the feasts and immorality of their culture chose to follow Jesus and joined the community of believers. Much of the meat sold in the meat market came from sacrifices offered to idols; some believers felt that they could not eat such meat in good conscience, so became vegetarian. Believers from Jewish backgrounds had the Sabbath day of rest built into their identity, and other special days in the Jewish calendar were important to them; but those days meant nothing to believers from Gentile backgrounds. Paul in this letter does not attempt to give instructions about what to eat or what days to observe; he is concerned about attitudes, and how to live in love with believers with whom we disagree strongly, believers whom we suspect do not have the strength of faith that they ought to have.

There are, again, positive and negative aspects to what Paul teaches. On the positive side, we are to receive one another as friends; on the negative side, we are not to judge or despise one another, assuming that God feels the same as we do. God has welcomed into his family all believers in Jesus, whether or not they hold the same views as us! And Paul emphasises that the primary relationship for each of us is with our Lord and Saviour Jesus: we all are serving him, seeking his honour and glory, we all are accountable to him, we all depend on him for salvation and strength to stand firm in our faith, we all give thanks to God for the blessings we sense he has given us. We are united with Christ; and if we are all united with Christ we are united with each other, in Christ. That unity needs to show. When there are disputes we need to think and pray about our position in the matters under consideration and reach a position of confidence and conviction, but always with humility and a non-judgemental attitude. Those who have reached a different conclusion may well be right! And since we are all united to Christ, we need to welcome one another as friends, in sincerity not pretence.

Our issues within the church today are not the same as those in Paul's day. At the time of writing we have had within my memory arguments about the language we use in our worship services, whether or not women should wear a covering on their heads, whether women should be in positions of leadership, whether divorced people can get remarried in church, and today whether gay people should have faithful sexual relationships and even get married in church, and what should be our attitude towards transgender people who are not happy with the gender assigned to them at birth. But the principles remain the same – be convinced in our own mind, but do not judge or despise faithful believers who have come to different conclusions: love them and receive them as friends.

[13]Let us, then, cease to judge one another. Rather let this be your resolve – never to place a stumbling-block or an obstacle in the way of a fellow follower of the Lord. [14]Through my union with the Lord Jesus, I know and am persuaded that nothing is defiling in itself. A thing is "defiling" only to the person who holds it to be so. [15]If, for the sake of what you eat, you wound your fellow follower's feelings, your life has ceased to be ruled by love. Do not, by what you eat, ruin someone for whom Christ died! [16]Do not let what is right for you become a matter of reproach. [17]For the kingdom of God does not consist of eating and drinking, but of righteousness and peace and gladness through the presence of the Holy Spirit. [18]The person who serves the Christ in this way pleases God, and wins the approval of their fellows. [19]Therefore our efforts should be directed towards all that makes for peace and the mutual building up of character. [20]Do not undo God's work for

the sake of what you eat. Though everything is "clean," yet, if a person eats so as to put a stumbling-block in the way of others, they do wrong. [21]The right course is to abstain from meat or wine or, indeed, anything that is a stumbling-block to your fellow follower of the Lord. [22]As for yourself – keep this conviction of yours to yourself, as in the presence of God. Happy the person who never has to condemn themselves in regard to something they think right! [23]The person, however, who has misgivings stands condemned if they still eat, because their doing so is not the result of faith. And anything not done as the result of faith is a sin.

I WONDER HOW MUCH OF our conversation with other Christians involves criticism – looking at mistakes, faults, weaknesses in one aspect or another of a person's life. Jesus' strongest condemnations were aimed at religious leaders and those who claimed to occupy the moral high ground – the Pharisees – whom he exposed as hypocrites; as his followers, should we be doing the same thing? How does this tie in with his teaching in the sermon on the mount not to judge one another? How does it tie in with Paul's teaching? In this passage he clearly echoes Jesus' teaching about not judging; yet in another passage (1 Corinthians 14) he tells us to exercise judgement – to weigh the words of those who claim to be passing on a message from God, so that we can hold on to what is good and reject what is wrong.

I suspect the answer lies in Jesus' words in Matthew 10:16: 'be wise as snakes, and as blameless as doves'. We need to be wise and see what is good and godly; and we need to avoid words or attitudes that harm people in any way. Paul here tells us not to place obstacles in the way of a fellow believer, not to wound their feelings or bring them down, but to build them up. That is being as blameless as doves. Earlier on he told us not to think of ourselves more highly than we ought to think (Romans 12:3); and in Philippians 2:3 he tells us, 'In humility lift others up above yourselves.' When we are talking about other believers' faults, it is difficult at the same time to be lifting them above ourselves! And if we are talking about them behind their backs, that is unlikely to result in them being built up, more likely to demean them. The Bible encourages us to talk to the person at fault in the hope of restoring them and building them up, but to do so in humility and in awareness of our own weaknesses (Galatians 6:1). It may wound their feelings for a time; but if it results in greater Christ-likeness, that pain would be worth it. When Jesus castigated the scribes and Pharisees, he did so in grief and love. When we have criticisms to make, we need the same attitude as Jesus.

Paul is happy to state his own beliefs in the matter of eating and drinking: 'nothing is defiling in itself', but 'only to the person who believes it to be so.' Nevertheless, if it is defiling to a person who believes it to be so, we need to do all in our power to prevent giving that person offence – not by argument (v. 1) or by brazenly seeming to defile ourselves in their eyes – that is not loving. 'Do not let what is right for you become a matter of reproach.' If we are called upon to give a reason for our actions, it is fine to do so – if done with humility and love. But our main motivation must be 'towards all that makes for peace and the mutual building up of character.' We seek first God's kingdom and his righteousness, and 'the kingdom of God does not consist of eating and drinking, but of righteousness and peace and gladness through the presence of the Holy Spirit.' That means biting our tongues on occasions!

Paul ends this section with a stark warning: 'Anything that is not done as a result of faith is sin.' It is important to be convinced in our own minds about controversial issues of Christian behaviour, for if we act in a way that we do not feel happy with, we are falling short of Christ-likeness – we sin. If we are sure we are doing the right thing, even if others are not sure, then that is great (providing we are not causing them offence). But if we are not sure, then don't do it!

All this gives me pause for much thought and prayer.

ROMANS CHAPTER 15

¹We, the strong, ought to take on our own shoulders the weaknesses of those who are not strong, and not merely to please ourselves. ²Let each of us please our neighbour for our neighbour's good, to help in the building up of their character. ³Even the Christ did not please himself! On the contrary, as scripture says of him – "The reproaches of those who were reproaching you fell upon me." ⁴Whatever was written in the scriptures in days gone by was written for our instruction, so that, through patient endurance, and through the encouragement drawn from the scriptures, we might hold fast to our hope. ⁵And may God, the giver of this patience and this encouragement, grant you to be united in sympathy in Christ, ⁶so that with one heart and one voice you may praise the God and Father of Jesus Christ, our Lord. ⁷Therefore always receive one another as friends, just as the Christ himself received us, to the glory of God.

Paul sums up his teaching, placing the onus of unity on those whose faith is strongest. This seems at first blush to be telling those with strong faith to hide it, and not to parade it in front of those who have not yet reached the same conclusions. And that, I think, is a necessary first step – we are aiming for our neighbour's good, to build them up, and that begins with love rather than teaching. When there is trust and respect on both sides, then matters of disagreement can be brought out into the open and examined without fear. But when our own pleasure and comfort or status comes first, that opens the door to hostility. Jesus is the one we follow, and his whole life was devoted to others rather than himself, even though obedience to his Father often resulted in blame from the people – Paul quotes Isaiah 45:23 to make his point.

The quotation from Scripture leads Paul on to making a general comment about Scripture (in his days, our Old Testament): it was all written for our instruction and encouragement, so that we might continue loving and serving God whatever our circumstances, believing that in the end we will receive what God has promised his people – a glorious place in the age to come, the new heaven and earth. This endurance and encouragement, coming to us through the Scriptures, has its origin in God – he is the giver of these blessings, for he is the one who inspired those Scriptures (see 2 Timothy 3:16). But how do we receive this encouragement? So often when we read the Scriptures, we don't feel we are getting much from them – especially if we are reading them only out of a sense of duty. It is worth asking how people like Paul, and even Jesus himself, read them. I suspect that they did so in simple faith that the words of Scripture were indeed the words of God. That would not stop them asking questions, comparing one Scripture with another to try to see the whole picture, and it certainly wouldn't stop them using their brains! I find that the more I read, the more I understand and the more I sense that God has indeed inspired them. I realise that reading them as if they were written by 21st Century authors is not helpful - they were written to strengthen our relationship with God, not to be read as text books of science or history. There's much I still don't understand, there are still many questions; but I don't think I am in a position to sit in judgement on them and say, 'This bit was inspired by God, but that bit was not.'

Paul then comes back to the topic he is really wanting to press home. Scripture reminded him that Jesus experienced reproach – he shared our experiences, and that is an encouragement to us when we find ourselves misunderstood and reproached. But the Scriptures also tell us of a glorious future, a future shared by those with weak faith as well as those who are strong. We all are on our way to the same destination! So Paul prays for unity in the community of believers, a unity of hearts and minds reflecting their unity in Christ, a unity which gets a voice in united praise to God.

Singing is a great way to praise God! I need to remind myself when singing worship hymns and songs to try to mean the words as I sing them, and to believe I am singing in the presence of the Lord (and all the hosts of heaven). I also need to remind myself to listen to other voices around me, and to believe that they too are doing the same thing in the same spirit. Some people use actions to supplement their voices – raising of hands, clapping, dancing. I am quite an introvert (really!), and such actions don't come naturally to me (even when watching football or rugby matches!); but I enjoy watching other people getting caught up in worship, and when I notice that they are focusing on God that encourages me to focus too. The tunes may not be to my taste, the words may not be what I would like to say at the moment, but I should not withdraw from worship on that account – there may be people present who really engage with them, and if they are being built up, that's great. We aim to please God, not ourselves; and God wants us to be united when worshipping him, even if that is difficult!

⁸For I tell you that Christ, in vindication of God's truthfulness, has become a minister of the covenant of circumcision, so that he may fulfil the promises made to our ancestors, ⁹and that the Gentiles also may praise God for his mercy. As scripture says – "Therefore will I make acknowledgment to you among the Gentiles and sing in honour of your name." ¹⁰And again it says – "Rejoice, you Gentiles, with God's people." ¹¹And yet again – "Praise the Lord, all you Gentiles, and let all Peoples sing his praises." ¹²Again, Isaiah says – "There will be a Scion of the house of Jesse, One who is to arise to rule the Gentiles; on him will the Gentiles rest their hopes." ¹³May God, who inspires our hope, grant you perfect happiness and peace in your faith, until you are filled with this hope by the power of the Holy Spirit.

I HAVE NOTICED THAT this translation sometimes says 'the Christ', and sometimes 'Christ'. The former sounds a bit odd to me – I am so used to using 'Christ' as a name. However, the word 'Christ' is the Greek version of the Hebrew word 'Messiah', and it is more natural to say 'the Messiah' than to use 'Messiah' as a name or an adjective, as in 'Jesus Messiah'. I think Paul's usage is reflecting a trend in the early church towards using 'Christ' as a name for

Jesus; but it always carried the meaning 'Messiah', 'anointed one' (the English version!), with all the feelings associated with that.

The Messiah, Jesus, has 'become a minister of the covenant of circumcision' (literally, 'a minister of circumcision'). Many translations take that to be a way of saying he became a minister for the Jews (Paul often uses the word circumcision as a synonym for the Jews). Yet his choice of that word reminds me that circumcision was given to Abraham as a sign of the covenant between him and his descendants and God, the covenant that God would be their God, and they would be his people (Genesis 17). Jesus, by his life, death and resurrection, has opened the way into God's presence, without which God could not be his people's God and they could not be his people. Thus Jesus vindicated God's truthfulness – the covenant of circumcision was given in anticipation of what Jesus would do.

Christ's work was not only for the Jews, as Paul has already made clear. It was also for Gentiles – the promise to Abraham was that he would be the father of many nations. So people of many nations can be included in God's covenant – a covenant of grace, for it depends on God's love, not on our ability to live godly lives. The Jewish Scriptures anticipated this – Paul quotes several of them. So Paul concludes this section with a prayer for all the Christians in Rome, whatever their background: 'May God, who inspires our hope, grant you perfect happiness and peace in your faith, until you are filled with this hope by the power of the Holy Spirit.'

I love his emphasis on hope! He wants everyone to be filled with hope as they look forward to the future – that glorious future which will never end. But he also wants them to enjoy the present as much as possible, with perfect happiness and peace in their faith. Some of his readers would be slaves, some would not be in the happiest of circumstances; yet alongside their difficulties and hurts there could be happiness and peace in their faith. Karl Marx famously described religion as the 'opiate of the masses'. There is some truth in that, if opiates control pain; but happiness and peace go hand in hand with not seeking one's own pleasures, and instead presenting our bodies to Christ as living sacrifices, with endurance and patience. Having hope, peace and happiness is no excuse for not trying to make the world a better place, even if that is costly! We are following Jesus 'who, for the joy that lay before him, endured the cross, heedless of its shame, and now "has taken his seat at the right hand" of the throne of God' (Hebrews 12:2); yet while facing the cross was able to say to his disciples, 'My own peace I give you' (John 14:27). God grants us happiness and peace in our faith; as we keep trusting Jesus and living in his light God grows our happiness and peace, and we find that we look forward more and more to the future he has promised us - we are being filled with hope. This is not the result of any spiritual exercise or discipline; it is the work of the Holy Spirit living in us as we live in union with Christ.

[14]I am persuaded, my friends – yes, I Paul, with regard to you – that you are yourselves full of kindness, furnished with all Christian learning, and well able to give advice to one another. [15]But in parts of this letter I have expressed myself somewhat boldly – by way of refreshing your memories – [16]because of the charge with which God has entrusted me, that I should be an

assistant of Christ Jesus to go to the Gentiles – that I should act as a priest of God's good news, so that the offering up of the Gentiles may be an acceptable sacrifice, consecrated by the Holy Spirit. [17]It is, then, through my union with Christ Jesus that I have a proud confidence in my work for God. [18]For I will not dare to speak of anything but what Christ has done through me to win the obedience of the Gentiles – [19]by my words and actions, through the power displayed in signs and marvels, and through the power of the Holy Spirit. And so, starting from Jerusalem and going as far as Illyria, I have told in full the good news of the Christ; [20]yet always with the ambition to tell the good news where Christ's name had not previously been heard, so as to avoid building on another's foundations. [21]But as scripture says – "They to whom he had never been proclaimed will see; and they who have never heard will understand!"

PAUL FINISHES HIS LETTER on a much more personal note. As he said at the beginning of this letter, he believes that the Christians in Rome have been taught well and have taken the good news of Jesus to heart. Yet he has felt compelled to write to them in this way ('refreshing your memories'!) because of the responsibility God has given him to take the gospel to the Gentiles. The word here translated 'charge' is literally 'grace' – what God has commanded him to do is not so much a burden, more a privilege. It is interesting how he uses the language of sacrifice here, 'so that the offering up of the Gentiles may be an acceptable sacrifice, consecrated by the Holy Spirit.' A sacrifice was something special given up to God, and that is how Paul sees the Gentile Christians: they were now special, chosen by God; they were sacrifices, who had given themselves wholly to Jesus, and they had been made acceptable by the Holy Spirit living in them and leading them into the truth. Paul is confident that Christ has been working through him in all the places he has preached about Jesus, and he glories in what Jesus is doing. Paul is an apostle, sent by God, he has taught about Jesus both by words and by his life, and he has seen God confirm his teaching by miracles which could only have been done by the Holy Spirit. Would that God was working in a similar way today in my own country! Miracles there are, I am sure, but not quite as they were in Paul's day!

Paul believed that God wanted him to preach the good news of Jesus to people who had never heard of him. Others could then build on the foundations he laid, but he didn't feel it was his job to build up churches which others had started – though maybe the church in Rome was an exception to his rule. And the success of his mission he sees foretold in the Scripture he quotes (from a Greek translation of Isaiah 52:15).

[22]That is why I have so often been prevented from coming to you. [23]But now there are no further openings for me in these parts, and I have for several years been longing to come to you whenever I may be going to Spain. [24]For my hope is to visit you on my journey, and then to be sent on my way by you, after I have first partly satisfied myself by seeing something of you.

^{25}Just now, however, I am on my way to Jerusalem, to take help to Christ's people there. ^{26}For Macedonia and Greece have been glad to make a collection for the poor among Christ's people at Jerusalem. ^{27}Yes, they were glad to do so; and indeed it is a duty which they owe to them. For the Gentile converts who have shared their spiritual blessings are in duty bound to minister to them in the things of this world. ^{28}When I have settled this matter, and have secured for the poor at Jerusalem the enjoyment of these benefits, I will go, by way of you, to Spain. ^{29}And I know that, when I come to you, it will be with a full measure of blessing from Christ.

THE OPEN DOORS FOR ministry that Paul found meant he hadn't had the opportunity to go to Rome. That opportunity had now come, since the gospel had spread as far as the region of Illyria, to the north west of Greece and Macedonia, a region which had become the Roman province of Illyricum. (That journey is not mentioned in the book of Acts.) Paul's ambition is to preach in Spain, a centre of Roman influence in the western Mediterranean, and his visit to Rome will be just a passing one, he hopes, though one full of blessing. (We don't know whether that ambition was ever fulfilled.) However, that plan would have to wait; just at the moment Paul was on the way to Jerusalem in an effort to relieve poor Christians in Jerusalem with funds he had collected on his journeys, especially in Macedonia and Greece – he talks about this extensively in his letters to the Corinthians. Here he simply mentions that the Gentiles in those regions were glad to help this effort, especially since they recognised that the blessings they were enjoying originated in Jerusalem. If those who give us spiritual blessing are themselves in need, we owe it to them to do what we can to help them.

> ³⁰I beg you, then, friends, by Jesus Christ, our Lord, and by the love inspired by the Spirit, to join me in earnest prayer to God on my behalf. ³¹Pray that I may be rescued from those in Judea who reject the faith, and that the help which I am taking to Jerusalem may prove acceptable to Christ's people; ³²so that, God willing, I may be able to come to you with a joyful heart, and enjoy some rest among you. ³³May God, the giver of peace, be with you all. Amen.

PAUL'S MENTION OF HIS visit to Jerusalem reminds him of the dangers he was likely to face, so he urgently asks them to pray for him. His request is given added emphasis by his appeal to Jesus and to Spirit-inspired love. He is aware that there were many in Judea who still nursed a grudge against him and wanted to see him dead, and he is not sure how the offering he is bringing would be received; he would love to go to Rome with a heart that was at ease and happy. In the end, his prayer was not answered in the way he wanted – he did arrive in Rome, but as a prisoner on his way to stand trial before Caesar, to whom he had appealed when his enemies in Judea hatched a plot to kill him.

Many people ask why we need to pray at all, since God already knows what we need and what we are going to say. And why involve other people in our prayers? Some Christians ask the Virgin Mary, or various saints, to pray for them; others will only ask living saints (the people of God) to pray for them. But most are happy to pray and be prayed for. I think one answer lies in this passage, in Paul's appeal to Jesus and to the love inspired by the Spirit: Jesus is the one with whom we are united as members of his body, and our unity is manifested in our love for one another, a love which is inspired by the Holy Spirit rather than by anything particularly loveable that we can see. Since we are united together, what affects one Christian affects us all, and just as the bits of our bodies unite to fight infection or a threat, so we unite in prayer. Jesus said that where two or three meet in his name he will be present, and that whatever we agree to ask will be granted, so this union in prayer is important. But this passage also shows us that even the most united and earnest prayer is not always answered in the way we expect or want, and often we don't know why that is, even in hindsight. We live by faith, and trust God even in the darkness.

Paul's final sentence in this chapter is itself a prayer: that God, the giver of peace, would be with all his readers. He adds 'Amen', a word usually showing agreement with a prayer someone else is praying; here it seems to be added simply for emphasis – he really does want God, the giver of peace, to be with them all. (I wonder if his scribe, Tertius, added it to show his agreement!) Whatever the reason, the prayer is a suitable one for this letter, for it is all about peace which is given us by God – peace with God through Jesus, and peace with one another. The word 'peace' is not just the absence of strife, but the presence of harmony and health. Ultimately it is the gift that will be given to the whole of creation, when everything in heaven and on earth is united under Christ (see Ephesians 1:10). Amen – so be it!

ROMANS CHAPTER 16

¹I commend to your care our sister, Phoebe, who is a minister of the church at Cenchreae; ²and I ask you to give her a Christian welcome – one worthy of Christ's people – and to aid her in any matter in which she may need your assistance. She has proved herself a staunch friend and protector to me and to many others.

Phoebe was almost certainly the one who brought this letter from Paul to Rome. We know nothing about her except what is written here; she was obviously a fairly significant person both in the church in Cenchreae (in Greece) and in the community – perhaps she was going to Rome on business. If she regularly travelled to Rome she would know what the state of Christianity was there, and that might account for Paul's information about which of his many friends would be in Rome when she got there – in those days all roads did seem to lead to Rome. (The long list of greetings that follow lead many scholars to think that Paul, who had not yet visited Rome, could not have known them; so they surmise that this chapter was an addition to the letter to Rome, perhaps added when a copy of the letter was sent elsewhere – Ephesus is a favourite suggestion. However, this point is argued about, and I'm happy to think that it was part of the original letter.)

³Give my greeting to Prisca and Aquila, my fellow workers in the cause of Christ Jesus, ⁴who risked their own lives to save mine. It is not I alone who thank them, but all the churches among the Gentiles thank them also. ⁵Give my greeting, also, to the church that meets at their house, as well as to my dear friend Epaenetus, one of the first in Roman Asia to believe in Christ; ⁶to Mary, who worked hard for you; ⁷to Andronicus and Junia, fellow Jews and once my fellow prisoners, who are people of note among the apostles, and who became Christians before I did; ⁸to my dear Christian friend Ampliatus; ⁹to Urban, our fellow worker in the cause of Christ, and to my dear friend Stachys; ¹⁰to that tried and true Christian Apelles; to the household of Aristobulus; ¹¹to my countryman Herodion; to the Christians in the household of Narcissus; ¹²to Tryphaena and Tryphosa, who have worked hard for the Master; to my dear friend Persis, for she has done much hard work for the Master; ¹³to that eminent Christian, Rufus, and to his mother, who has been a mother to me also; ¹⁴to Asyncritus, Phlegon, Hermes, Patrobas, Hermas, and our friends with them; ¹⁵also to Philologus and Julia, Nereus and his sister, and Olympas, and to all Christ's people who are with them. ¹⁶Greet one another

with a sacred kiss. All the churches of the Christ send
you greetings.

WE KNOW OF SOME OF these people from other parts of
the Bible such as Acts. Prisca (short for Priscilla) and Aquila had
been expelled from Rome when the emperor Claudius expelled all
the Jews; but many came back when it was safe, and Prisca and
Aquila may well have been among them. There is plenty of room
for speculation! Some are commended for their good work; others
are just names. Junia is interesting, as being a woman of note among
the apostles – some scholars can't believe she was a woman, and
that the name should be Junias, but there is no record of such
a name. What strikes me is the number of friends Paul had, and
wanted to ensure they knew he was thinking about them. Many
people these days think Paul was a bit of a misogynist, and that he
must have been very stern and unloving; but this list – and, indeed,
the whole of this letter – portrays him as a very loving, caring
person to both men and women. He ends this list of greetings with
a general instruction to greet one another in the usual way – a kiss
– but to make sure that it is a Christian greeting, with no unwanted
connotations! And he sends greetings from all the churches he was
visiting at the time, a reminder that there is in fact only one church,
united in Jesus.

17I beg you, friends, to be on your guard against people
who, by disregarding the teaching which you received,
cause divisions and create difficulties; dissociate
yourselves from them. 18For such persons are not

serving Christ, our Master, but are slaves to their own appetites; and, by their smooth words and flattery, they deceive simple-minded people. [19]Everyone has heard of your ready obedience. It is true that I am very happy about you, but I want you to be well versed in all that is good, and innocent of all that is bad. [20]And God, the giver of peace, will before long crush Satan under your feet.

May the blessing of Jesus, our Lord, be with you.

IN THIS PERSONAL SECTION Paul can't help warning the Christians in Rome against those who cause divisions and create difficulties. The instructions about unity and love could easily have been taken to mean welcoming people whoever they were, even those who would hinder their life as followers of Jesus. We have a vicious and clever spiritual enemy in the form of Satan, the devil, and we need to be on our guard against his evil plans. Jesus has defeated him, and when Jesus returns to earth he will be dealt with once and for all; but until that day we do need to be alert to his temptations, and to the fact that he often uses people who claim to be Christian to serve his purposes. Loving unity is not served by those who cause division, so Paul tells his Roman readers not to associate with such people. How did they cause divisions? We don't know; but Paul's instructions about the Christian life in the last few chapters all promote unity and peace, and we can guess that those divisive people used their smooth words to criticise and condemn those with whom they disagreed, and to promote their own 'strong faith' at the expense of the unity Paul – and Jesus – wanted. Paul had occasion to warn the Christians in Corinth about their tendency to form factions (1 Corinthians 3 and 4), and about 'super-apostles' (2 Corinthians 11), and much later John had to warn against a guy called Diotrephes (3 John). Disunity was a problem in the early church. How much worse it is today! Is our love of truth and purity trumping our love for our fellow believers, with whom we are united in Christ?

²¹Timothy, my fellow worker, sends you his greetings, and Lucius, Jason, and Sosipater, my countrymen, send theirs.

²²I Tertius, who am writing this letter, send you my Christian greeting.

²³My host Gaius, who extends his hospitality to the whole church, sends you his greeting; and Erastus, the city treasurer, and Quartus, our dear friend, add theirs. ²⁴Note: Some later manuscripts add: The grace of our Lord Jesus Christ be with you all. Amen.

²⁵Now to him who is able to strengthen you, as promised in the good news entrusted to me and in the proclamation of Jesus Christ, in accordance with the revelation of that hidden purpose, which in past ages was kept secret but now has been revealed ²⁶and, in obedience to the command of the immortal God, made known through the writings of the prophets to all

nations, to secure submission to the faith – [27] to him, I say, the wise and only God, be ascribed, through Jesus Christ, all glory for ever and ever. Amen.

PAUL ADDS TO HIS GREETINGS those of his companions – Tertius, Paul's scribe who wrote the letter at Paul's dictation, adds his own greeting. (Verse 24 was added to later copies of the letter and was probably not part of the original, but found its way into the King James version of the Bible.)

The letter ends with a 'doxology', praise to God (which some scholars think was another addition to the letter, not written by Paul). It is worth looking at. Paul's good news is all about Jesus Christ, and it needs to be proclaimed; how can people hear unless they are told? This good news enables believers to stand firm – firmly believing the hope that it brings, firm in their relationship of love for God and trust in him, firm in their unity with God and each other. All this is in accordance with the revelation of God's hidden purpose, his purpose to bring peace with God to people of every nation. This purpose had been spoken about by the prophets, but was hidden from the Jews' understanding so that they tended to regard everyone else as outside God's love. However, God had revealed that purpose through Jesus to Paul and the other apostles, and they were commanded by 'the immortal God' to tell all the world. God is not like any of the gods of Rome or Greece or anywhere else; he is from everlasting to everlasting, and the whole world belongs to him. Peace with God, however, needs submission to the faith – when we believe in Jesus our relationship with God is restored, but our relationship has to be with God as he truly is: the wise and only God, the most important Being there is, the creator and rightful Lord of all in heaven and in the universe, our loving

Father. God is worthy of all honour and praise, and that is what Paul gives him now and wants us to give him too – through Jesus Christ, who has given us access into the presence of God. What a summary of Paul's teaching!

How do we give God the glory he deserves? Humanly speaking, it is impossible; but the Holy Spirit inspires us, and through our union with Jesus our weak and beggarly praise is seen as acceptable, even delightful, to God. When we are given our new bodies, immortal and perfect, we will be able to praise him perfectly; but even now, in this life, we can praise him in worship and prayer, in songs and music and dance, and in the silent adoration of our hearts. God is worthy of our praise! He is the giver of peace, peace at a terrible price to himself and his only Son, peace above all with himself, a peace which is bringing us to share in his glory. All because he loves us so much! To him indeed be ascribed all glory for ever and ever through Jesus Christ our Saviour and Lord. Amen!

About the Author

Tim Britton was born in Nigeria to British parents, and educated in England before getting a B.Sc. from Dundee University in Scotland. He went to Trinity College in Bristol, England, to study theology before ordination as a minister in the Church of England. While there he married Frances, whom he had met in Scotland, and they have two sons, both married with three children. Tim served in Norfolk, England, before the family went to Uganda to do missionary work. On their return to England he led parishes in Coventry and Warwickshire, England, before retiring to the North Norfolk coast. He has co-authored a course on basic Christian teaching for churches in Uganda.

Milton Keynes UK
Ingram Content Group UK Ltd.
UKHW011855161123
432711UK00001B/58